UFFA

Yachting's Eccentric Genius

Malcolm Turner

SunRise

First published in Great Britain in 2023 by SunRise

SunRise Publishing Ltd
124 City Road
London EC1V 2NX

ISBN 978-1-9144893-5-8

A CIP catalogue record for this book is available from the British Library.

Typeset in Minion Pro and Impact.
Printed by Bell & Bain Ltd, Glasgow

Contents

CHAPTER ONE: A Meeting of Minds   7

CHAPTER TWO: The Durbar Room   12

CHAPTER THREE: Valhalla   33

CHAPTER FOUR: Typhoon   41

CHAPTER FIVE: Radiant   55

CHAPTER SIX: Avenger   72

CHAPTER SEVEN: Sailing Canoes   102

CHAPTER EIGHT: Twenty Acres   117

CHAPTER NINE: The Airborne Lifeboat   133

CHAPTER TEN: Puckaster   154

CHAPTER ELEVEN: The Flying Fifteen   186

CHAPTER TWELVE: The Loveliest Music on Earth   210

ACKNOWLEDGEMENTS   246

BIBLIOGRAPHY   247

INDEX   248

You see things; and you say, 'Why?' But I dream things that never were; and I say, 'Why not?'

George Bernard Shaw: *Back to Methuselah*

They were built with the precision and artistry of a violin; Uffa had set new standards of workmanship in boatbuilding, and to own one of his fourteen-footers in the 1930s was to own the most perfect little boat in the world.

Sir Peter Scott: *The Eye of the Wind*

Chapter 1
A Meeting of Minds

It had been a wearying evening for the Duke of Edinburgh. After a lengthy round of introductions, he sighed, 'Isn't there anyone *interesting* here I can talk to?' Jimmy Damant, Commodore of the Island Sailing Club, looked hopefully around the dinner guests until his eyes fell upon his old friend, Uffa Fox. 'Oh yes,' said Jimmy, 'I know just the man.'[1]

The Club had given Elizabeth and Philip a Dragon yacht, *Bluebottle*, as a wedding present. The Dragon was, and remains, a popular One-Design keelboat that would soon be accepted as an Olympic Class.[2] Uffa had just launched his own One-Design—the Flying Fifteen—and he immediately invited Philip to sail with him in the prototype, *My Dainty Duck*. The next day, the duke was to discover what thousands of sailors would learn in the years to come. Uffa had achieved the Holy Grail of yacht racing: a keelboat that handled like a dinghy. Philip loved it and immediately asked Uffa to build one for him (number 192, *Coweslip*, was eventually given to Elizabeth and Philip as a present from the people of Cowes). When the duke and his entourage turned to leave, Uffa made

---

1   Interview with Tony Dixon, BBC South Today, 12 July 2012.
2   One-Design is a standardised racing class in which the first boat to finish wins the race, as opposed to handicap racing.

his usual offer to a new customer, 'Fancy a pint?' Philip, without hesitation, said he did and Uffa led the group across the road.

Cowes is a small place and word had quickly spread that Philip, accompanied by Uffa Fox, was about the town. The crowd which gathered might have expected them to go to a smart yacht club, or hotel, but Uffa headed directly to his local. The Duke of York was (and remains) an unpretentious pub, popular with boatbuilders, sailmakers and artisans from the yards around the Medina River. Uffa liked the fact that it was opposite his works, and he got easy credit terms from the landlord, Harry Wingham, who didn't press too hard for settlement.

Mrs Wingham had come outside with a group of her regulars to see what the commotion was about. She was left speechless when Uffa strode up to her and said, 'Get yourself back inside, missus, we're coming in.'[3] Her husband, who'd been about to drive away, abandoned his car in the middle of Mill Hill Road and rushed back, causing a traffic jam which brought Cowes to a standstill.

So began a lifelong friendship between two characters who—at first glance—could hardly have been more different. In background, rank, age and even appearance they were poles apart. Beneath the surface, however, they shared a ribald sense of humour, a dislike of pomposity and an unbounded appetite for life and fun. Often unguarded in their opinions and rarely mincing their words, they were connected by more than a love of sailing and the sea. Decades later, following Uffa's death, Philip would write: 'His life was one long campaign against the foolish, the stupid and the self-important, the whole conducted with a cheerful breeziness that disarmed all but the hardest cases. All the qualities of his nature were over life-size but neither malice nor dishonesty were among them.'[4]

3   Dixon, June, *UFFA FOX: A Personal Biography*, Angus & Robertson, 1978.
4   Ibid.

A Meeting of Minds

Philip had married Princess Elizabeth just a few months before meeting Uffa and neither the public nor the Court of St James's had immediately taken to him. A newspaper poll found that forty per cent of their readers objected to Elizabeth marrying a 'foreigner'. Senior members of the royal household were known to dislike him and some of King George VI's friends had privately dubbed him 'Charley Kraut'.[5]

He had endured a difficult childhood; his mother's depression led to a seven-year separation from her son, while his father decamped to France with his mistress. All four of his sisters had married German princes—two of whom were Nazis—and Philip was left to grow up almost alone in Britain. If that were not enough, the sister he was closest to, Cecille, was killed in an air crash in 1937.

Small wonder that he earned a reputation for being prickly and defensive. Even when he was sailing at Cowes Week, the 'foreign' label endured. During one race, the skipper of a nearby boat demanded right of way by calling 'Water!' When Philip did not immediately respond, there was a further call of 'Water, Stavros!' Philip shouted back: 'It's not Stavros and it's my wife's fucking water and I'll do what I fucking please.'[6]

A different duke might have been wary of friendship with such a maverick as Uffa but, away from the Court, Philip was determined to be his own man and that included choosing his own friends. Uffa had been famous since his twenties. Between the two World Wars, he had revolutionised sailing by designing and building planing dinghies that were infinitely faster than the older, heavier boats that had dominated racing since the late nineteenth century. In 1928, *Avenger*, his first successful planing design, had earned him fifty-two firsts, two seconds and three thirds out of fifty-seven starts. *Avenger* also won him the Prince of Wales Cup, then the most coveted trophy in dinghy racing. Later that year, almost on an impulse, he sailed

---

5   Lloyd, Ian, *The Duke*, The History Press, 2021.
6   *Daily Mail*, 8 June 2009.

Avenger to France, itself a remarkable feat in an open boat only fourteen feet long with a displacement of 800 pounds.

In Le Havre, he raced and beat the French fleet. The city fêted him everywhere, and his reputation began to spread internationally. Before long, he had become the most celebrated and successful yacht designer in the world. In the years since his death his reputation has grown rather than diminished. The Flying Fifteen alone has become the largest fixed-keel class in the world, with over 4,000 boats regularly competing across many countries.

Uffa, however, was always more than a sailor and boat designer. He was a multifaceted force of nature with an original mind and limitless energy for whatever new idea seized his imagination. He was also an irrepressible extrovert and novel thinker, as well as a singer, musician, journalist, author, painter, sportsman, countryman, campaigner, controversial businessman and friend of royalty. No one who came across Uffa ever forgot him, even if it was only from the far side of a room. 'He was such a character, you know, whenever you went out to dinner with him to a restaurant, he seemed to just take the restaurant over and get everyone singing and listening to his stories.'[7]

Despite the popularity of his designs, his chaotic finances meant that he made little money from them. In 1934, he published his first book, *Sailing, Seamanship and Yacht Construction*. It was an immediate success and added a much-needed supplement to his income. He would continue to write and publish for the rest of his life, usually pleasing both critics and public alike. His readers soon discovered that Uffa's books were much more than discourses on naval architecture. At their best, they came close to poetry. Here is Uffa writing about one of his favourite boats, his twenty-ton schooner, the *Black Rose*: '... between the main and

7   Kerley, Lisa. *Memories of the Sea—Interview with Tony Dixon*. 29th August 2018.

foremasts she set a wonderful main-topmast staysail, that floated aloft like a cloud and seemed to rake all the winds out of heaven. The hull flared off above water forward to throw away flying spray, and amidships and aft she tumbled home to ease the deck lines when she was hard pressed with her lee decks awash.'[8]

Uffa Fox was a Universal Man who not only changed his sport, his Island and the lives of his friends, he left an unfillable void. Such people are rare, and his story deserves to be remembered.

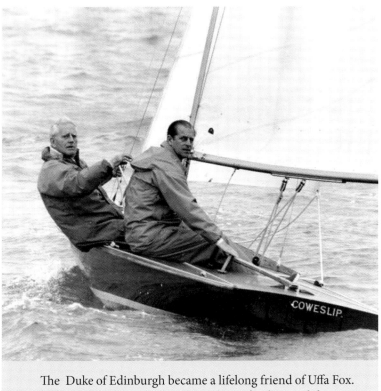

The Duke of Edinburgh became a lifelong friend of Uffa Fox. The two men shared more than a love of sailing and the sea.

---

8   Fox, Uffa, *Joys of Life*, Newnes, 1966.

Chapter 2
The Durbar Room

U ffa Fox was born on 15 January 1898 at 2 Osborne Road, East Cowes. It would be hard to find a town more closely linked to the sea and seafaring. Cowes is the principal seaport of a small but strategically vital island which guards the entrance not only to the Royal Navy's home in Portsmouth, but also Britain's vital commercial port, Southampton.[9] Ships have been built there since Tudor times, and from the early nineteenth century Cowes has been a centre for international yacht racing. George IV was the first of many royal patrons, and the Cowes Week annual regatta remains the oldest and most respected in the world.

He was the second of three surviving children, arriving between an older sister, Mahala, and a younger sister, Elfrida. Two earlier children—Herbert and Dorothea—had died from diphtheria, and Elfrida would face a long struggle with poor health.[10] Although there was a high infant mortality rate in many late Victorian cities, the Isle of Wight was comparatively healthy with only ninety children from a population of

9   In recent times the port of Felixstowe has become Britain's busiest for containerised traffic.
10   Dixon, June, *UFFA FOX: A Personal Biography*, Angus & Robertson, 1978.

Uffa Fox was born at 2 Osborne Road, East Cowes, in the closing years of the nineteenth-century.

around 80,000 dying in that year.[11] Diphtheria, however, was highly contagious, largely untreatable before antibiotics, and the survival rate was barely fifty per cent.

Uffa's father, Arthur Fox, was a master carpenter who had worked on the teak carvings in the splendid Durbar Room at nearby Osborne House. He had learnt his trade as an

11   www.populationspast.org

apprentice boatbuilder and joiner at John Samuel White's shipyard in Cowes,[12] later going to sea as a ship's carpenter on the liners of the Peninsula and Orient line.

There had been mariners in the family for generations. Uffa's great-grandfather, William (Joe) Miller, had been a merchant sea captain, and boatswain of the ill-fated HMS *Avenger*, a paddle wheel frigate which foundered on rocks near Malta in 1847. Miller, who perished along with most of the crew,[13] was so highly regarded that he was given a lengthy obituary in the *Illustrated London News* and lauded as 'the very *beau idéal* of a British sailor.'[14]

Joe Miller was tall, powerfully built, handsome and charming, and he had married Elizabeth Roberton from a well-known Cowes family. Legend has it that, on returning from his voyages, he would fill her apron with gold sovereigns. He had been at sea from the age of eleven, and had served in the Merchant Navy, Royal Navy and United States Navy, where he had seen action in hand-to-hand fighting. While sailing on a whaler, he had been taken prisoner by Native Americans and, when serving as a mercenary in the Chilean Navy, had been the first to board the Spanish flag ship, *Esmeralda*, personally decapitating the only man to oppose him. His premature death left Elizabeth to raise their two children alone. She never got over the loss of her husband and, like Queen Victoria, she wore widow's weeds for the rest of her life. Mahala Fox would remember her as 'a very sad old lady dressed in black.'[15] One of Joe's two daughters, Mary Jane, married John Fox who had left his native Lincolnshire for Cowes to work as Head Carpenter to Queen Victoria

---

12   There were two shipyards known as 'Whites' in Cowes at that time: J Samuel White (1815–1981) and William White & Sons (1883–1929). The present Wight Shipyard Co (WSC) began life in 2010 as Shemara Refit LLP.
13   There were only eight survivors from a crew of 250.
14   *Illustrated London News*, 29 January 1848.
15   Dixon, June, *UFFA FOX: A Personal Biography*, Angus & Robertson, 1978.

The loss of HM Steam Frigate Avenger, *Captain Charles Napier,
off the Coast of Barbary on the night of 20 December, 1847.*
C P Williams.

at Osborne House, thus establishing the Fox name on the Isle of Wight. Small wonder that Uffa always dreamt of an adventurous life at sea.

Uffa's mother, Eliza Fox (née Cobbold), was known to her friends as Lucy. She came from Suffolk farming stock and had met Arthur while working as a housekeeper for Queen Victoria at Osborne House. Scandinavian names for both people and places have survived in some parts of East Anglia, and she was following a family tradition by naming her children Mahala, Uffa and Elfrida. It was not by chance that Arthur and Lucy had each found senior positions in the royal household. Both were hard working, diligent and reliable. Lucy was so trusted that she was placed in charge of an annexe to Osborne House which the queen used to entertain her most important royal and diplomatic guests.[16]

Domestic service could be a harsh and unforgiving

16   Dixon, June, *UFFA FOX: A Personal Biography*, Angus & Robertson, 1978

environment in the late nineteenth century, but Queen Victoria and Prince Albert sought to be model employers. Albert was a reformer and patron of art and industry. He had methodically reorganised the royal household, ensuring that it operated within a strict budget, and he took pains to hire the best-trained and most efficient staff. He knew that it mattered: earlier mistakes had caused a public scandal for Victoria during the 'Bedchamber Crisis' of 1839.[17] Some historians have attributed the survival of British constitutional monarchy into the twenty-first century to Albert's influence.

Arthur and Lucy Fox had briefly lived in London while Arthur worked as a woodcarver at Westminster Abbey, but returned to Cowes before they had children. As often happens with Island people, they did not find mainland life to their taste. Uffa probably encapsulated their feelings when he later wrote of his own experiences: 'I tried to live in London once, and in America twice. Six months was all I could stay in London and four months only was all I could endure in the United States, before the magic of the Island drew me home again.'[18]

Arthur and Lucy Fox had enough money saved (with a little help from relatives) to buy their own home, a four-bedroom, semi-detached house in the centre of East Cowes. Uffa was born into a secure, comfortable and moderately affluent family. His paternal grandfather, John Fox, lived around the corner in York Avenue and was a prominent member of the nearby Anglican church, St James. In addition to shrewdness with money and property, Arthur would also inherit some freeholds. In a 2017 interview, Tony Dixon (Uffa's nephew), recalled that Arthur later became a rate collector for the council and owned many of the houses in Mayfield Avenue, the street that the Fox family would later move to.

Uffa's great-grandfather Roberton had been granted

---

17   Queen Victoria was fond of her Whig prime minister, Lord Melbourne, and she declined Robert Peel's demand to have Tory ladies in waiting in her household. Peel consequently refused to become prime minister, prompting a constitutional crisis.
18   Fox, Uffa, *Joys of Life,* Newnes, 1966.

sole ferry rights across the Medina, the river which divides East and West Cowes. According to the family legend, the Governor of the Isle of Wight had made a wager that he could ride around the circumference of the Island on horseback but faced defeat when he reached the Medina River. The fierce tide and deep water made it impossible for him to ride across, and the rules of the wager meant that he could not dismount. Uffa's great-grandfather is believed to have lashed two rowing boats together, placed the horse's forelegs in one and the hindlegs in the other, and then rowed the two boats across while the governor remained in the saddle. The wager was duly won, and great-grand-father Roberton was rewarded with the ferry rights.

This was a valuable franchise because there has never been a permanent bridge or tunnel and, to this day, the two halves of the town are connected only by a chain ferry known as the 'Floating Bridge' (the alternative being a forty-kilometre detour via Newport). Roberton later sold the rights to the Southampton Isle of Wight and South of England Royal Mail Steam Packet Company in exchange for a pension.[19] One of Uffa's uncles, William Hillyer, then the manager of Bannister's Rope Works, persuaded the Reverend Prothero, Vicar of St James's, to sign a certificate confirming that Roberton was alive long after he had actually died.[20] This enabled the family to draw the annuity for many more years. Entrepreneurship, opportunism and a disregard for inconvenient rules were long-established traits of the Fox clan.

Uffa's earliest memory was of Queen Victoria's funeral cortège passing his grandfather's house in 1901. He was only three, but the death of the queen had cast a long shadow over

---

19   The Southampton Isle of Wight and South of England Royal Mail Steam Packet Company is Britain's longest surviving ferry company and was once the longest name in the records of Companies House. Today the company is known simply as Red Funnel.

20   Dixon, June, *UFFA FOX: A Personal Biography*, Angus & Robertson, 1978.

a town that feared for its future. The presence of the royal family in nearby Osborne House had brought prosperity, status and many well-paid jobs, not least within the Fox household. The fears were well-founded; Edward VII had never liked Osborne and he quickly 'gave it to the nation', initially as a naval college.

Uffa recalled, 'After the procession down York Avenue, we went to the grounds of Norris Castle to view the royal yacht *Alberta,* with the late queen in her coffin, pass through the long lines of men-o'-war, which then fired their last salute. On this sad occasion, as so often, the wind was westerly, and the sky overcast, but as the royal yacht, on leaving Cowes Roads, changed her course from north to east, the sun broke through the clouds and a great gleaming sunbeam fell full upon the *Alberta,* making her stand out brightly from all the sea and surrounding ships. I remember that this symbol from above deeply affected us all and especially my grandfather to whom there is a memorial tablet in St James's church for his fifty years' service to it.'[21]

From the moment of his birth, Lucy would dote on her only son and fiercely defend him from the least criticism. His father would be a role model, counsellor and occasional disciplinarian, but his mother would always envelope him in unconditional love and praise. He may have had her to thank for his unbounded optimism, self-belief, and determination to succeed.

Uffa's generation was the last to live without electricity, telephones, or radio in their homes. Even gramophones were expensive and rare, although his family did have an Edison phonograph on which they could make recordings on a reusable wax cylinder. He attributed, in part, his happy, confident childhood to the absence of technology and later feared the age of the computer, which he thought would only confuse future children.

---

21   Fox, Uffa, *Joys of Life,* Newnes, 1966.

HMY *Alberta* Entering Portsmouth Harbour with the Body
of Queen Victoria, 1 February 1901.
By William Lionel Wylliea.

No child, however, could grow up in Cowes without being
aware of the sea and hearing the tales of returning seamen.
His own home was filled with the ornaments his father had
brought back from voyages to the Far East. They included
exotic shells in which he could hear the sea, and a porcelain
woman from Japan who would fan herself if you gently
touched her arm.[22] Arthur Fox liked to sing sea shanties,
and Uffa, in turn, would collect and sing them for the rest
of his life. At the age of ten, Uffa's father presented him with
an inlaid cigarette holder, which he had brought home from
Japan, and gave him permission to smoke, but only with a
cigarette holder. Uffa, however, disliked cigarettes and never
smoked at any point in his life.

Uffa was, unmistakably, a man of his Island. He never
made any attempt to conceal his broad Isle of Wight accent,

---

22   Dixon, June, *UFFA FOX: A Personal Biography*, Angus &
Robertson, 1978.

and for all of his eccentricity, he was, first and foremost, a Caulkhead.[23][24] As is often the case in island communities, Isle of Wight people are generally close-knit, interdependent and, with a few exceptions, honest and generous. As Uffa himself put it, 'I have always believed that life on an island is happier than in a large place, for we cannot deceive each other. We all know each other's ancestry, the number of horses, cows, pigs, fields of wheat, barley and grazing fields each farmer has so there is no attempt at deceit. We know full well that unless we are fair and friendly no one will stretch out a helping hand to us in our time of need.'[25] In his speech and in his writing, he often referred to the mainland as 'England', and only half in jest.[26]

Island people live closer to nature, the weather and the changing moods of the sea than others, and religion is often important to them. Throughout his life, Uffa maintained a staunch Anglican faith and an unwavering belief in the afterlife or, as he preferred to call it, Paradise. When he knew that his own end was approaching, he wrote, 'So when death's dark angel glides silently invisible alongside, to bear my innermost spirit aloft, I shall go happily and shall not flinch.'[27]

Uffa would spend many happy summer holidays on Grandfather Cobbold's Woodhouse Farm, in Rattlesden, Suffolk. Usually staying for a month or longer at a time, the family would often be there for the harvest. At that time, wheat was still scythed either by hand or by horse-drawn cutters. In

---

23   The Isle of Wight accent is similar to the Hampshire accent, but a little rounder with some dropped consonants and longer vowels. Many words are unique to the Island, including chine (ravine).

24   A Caulkhead is a native of the Isle of Wight. In the past, islanders took seasonal work on the mainland, caulking (waterproofing) the hulls of boats.

25   Fox, Uffa. *Joys of Life*, Newnes 1966.

26   In his letters, Uffa would joke that Great Britain was 'an ally of ours'.

27   Fox, Uffa. *More Joys of Living*, Nautical Publishing Company, 1972.

later life, Uffa fondly remembered helping to stack the sheaves while men shot at the scattering rabbits. Recollections of long summer days in the fields, with one of his mother's fine cold lunches in a drawstring bag, nourished Uffa's enduring love of the country. When asked to name a newborn foal, he precociously dubbed it William Shakespeare: 'Even at that age I was beginning to appreciate his wonderous works, and this horse was christened the last week of our stay that summer.'[28] Coming home in the late evening, they would have tea by candlelight: 'Tea was a great and friendly meal, with everyone yarning, and all the stories were much more romantic when told in the ever-changing power of the light from candles, which continually altered the look of the face of the person telling the story and those listening to it.'[29]

During one holiday, he designed and built his first boat using a galvanised metal bath, which he took from the house. Rigging up a mast and sprit from bean sticks and using a shovel for a rudder, he made a foresail and a headsail from cotton cloth and launched it on the duck pond. He capsized before reaching the far bank, and later claimed that an unforeseen squall had caused him to founder. The family laughed but, as a punishment, made him clean both the bath and the cotton, following which the voyage became a family legend. The love of nature and the country which grew from those holidays came second only to his infatuation with the sea. Rural pursuits became lifelong passions, and he would never be entirely comfortable in any town larger than Cowes or Newport.

In 1903 there was a grand review of warships at Spithead. Uffa attributed his fascination with the sea and his determination to become a sailor to seeing the many men-o'-war and other ships that paraded in the Solent before being inspected by the king. He was given a wooden model of a man-o'-war to

---

28   Fox, Uffa, *Joys of Life*, Newnes, 1966.
29   Ibid.

float in his bath and it fired his fertile imagination. At a very early age the idea took hold that he would, one day, work with ships and the sea.

All three Fox children attended Whippingham School, which was a two-mile walk from their home in East Cowes. The school was selective, and Uffa and his siblings were given places following an interview which they walked to. Rebuilt in 1864, this was no ordinary village institution. There had been a school of sorts on the site since 1840, but Prince Albert, who was passionate about educational reform, had personally redesigned Whippingham as a model foundation where the children of Osborne's staff would be educated to a high standard. The new building had fine views south-west to the Medina River, and the teachers were handpicked from across the country. In Uffa's time, the headmaster held a PhD, a rare distinction for a village schoolmaster in Edwardian England. Prince Albert died before the new school building was complete, but the architect, A J Humbert, had worked closely to Albert's ideas. The four-mile round trip was thought to be good for the children but, when the weather was bad, Princess Beatrice (Victoria's daughter and Governor of the Isle of Wight) provided a horse-drawn brake.[30]

Uffa had a quick, enquiring mind and a highly retentive memory, but the walk to school through fields, woods and meadows appealed to him more than the lessons. When in the classroom, he was rebellious, distracted and continually in trouble. He would later write, 'I was an unruly boy who delighted in swimming, rowing, fishing, sailing, football, cricket, shooting, boxing, horses, cross-country running and such things.'[31] Those things, however, did not include homework, study, scholarship or even sitting quietly and attentively in class. Each morning his mother gave him a lunch bag packed with food fit for a king. Decades later he

30   Dixon, June, *UFFA FOX: A Personal Biography*, Angus & Robertson, 1978.
31   Fox, Uffa. *Joys of Life*. Newnes. 1966.

would recall, 'I shall never forget the wondrous food with which my mother filled my school satchel. Such delicacies as cold baked rice pudding, cold lobster, cold crab, sandwiches of wonderful, underdone red beef, a half of chicken, a partridge or pheasant and every so often a steak and kidney pudding, which I had to warm up. Although I loved this at home, I did not like it so much at school as I could not eat in class.'[32]

These feasts quickly led Uffa into trouble. Rather than wait for the lunch break, he would surreptitiously dine from his desk when he thought the master wasn't looking. He soon got caught and the meal was confiscated, but when the headmaster—Dr J W Rogerson—forgot to return it, a furious Lucy Fox descended on the school and gave him a memorable tongue-lashing, accusing him of eating the lunch himself.

Lucy had a blind spot where Uffa was concerned, and fiercely defended him whenever he was in trouble, which was much of the time. The chastened headmaster took Uffa aside a few days later and offered a compromise: the food would not be confiscated if Uffa was not seen eating it. From that day, the headmaster took care to make plenty of noise before entering the classroom and Uffa retained his wondrous meals. Dr Rogerson became a friend and personally coached Uffa in music and on the cricket pitch, leading to a lifelong love of sport, especially cricket. In time, Uffa would develop an unorthodox style but become an effective batsman. Throughout his schooldays he was, for most of the time, captain of both football and cricket and stroke of the rowing team. He was always competitive, and when his football team were defeated by another school by the humiliating margin of ten goals to one, it stung him deeply. He nursed a grudge until he was able to defeat the same school at cricket a few months later. 'Our revenge was glorious and once more we could hold our heads high.'[33]

Later in life, Uffa was asked to join a scratch eleven from Northwood Cricket Club, who were due to play a touring

---

32   Fox, Uffa. *Joys of Life*, Newnes 1966.
33   Ibid.

team of Oxford and Cambridge blues. On the way to the match, he stopped for a pint at The Granville pub, and took note of the motto above the bar: *Nil Desperandum*.[34] Uffa batted ferociously, trying to knock every ball clean out of the ground. In no time he was clocking up fours and sixes, pausing after each one to play his bat like a banjo and singing a ditty while the fielders retrieved the ball. He finally got caught out after ninety-eight runs. The opposing captain told him he'd never seen anyone play such terrible cricket and make so many runs so fast.[35]

East Cowes is a small town and the Isle of Wight, then and now, is largely rural. Uffa was always deeply attached to the countryside, as well as its flora, fauna and traditions. He adored animals, and kept pets throughout his life, beginning with his two ferrets, Jack and Jill, who travelled in his pocket and sat on his shoulder at mealtimes. He knew and loved every corner of his Island and was passionate about fishing, shooting, riding, rambling and practically everything connected with rural life. In time, he would become a recognised authority and would publish regular articles in *The Field, Country Life, Shooting Times* and other field sport and country publications.

In Uffa's youth, trading vessels still moored as far up the Medina River as Newport, and *The Bee*—a round-bilged, double-ended sailing ketch built before the Battle of Trafalgar— was the first boat he ever fell in love with. He and his friends would clamber over her decks and help the crew with the sails and rigging.

In East Cowes, the royal yacht *Britannia* would be laid up, always in the same berth, with a mighty felled oak lying beside her, should she ever need a new mast. On one occasion, when she was dismasted in a race, local shipwrights and riggers worked through the night to carve out a replacement, which they stepped, and rerigged before dawn. *Britannia* was race-

---

34   'Do not despair', attributed to Horace (68–65 BC).
35   Fox, Uffa, *Joys of Life*, Newnes, 1966.

HMY *Britannia* at Marvin's boatyard in East Cowes.

ready by 10:00 am the following morning. Cowes has always been proud of its royal connections.[36]

As an adult, he would often attend the Tuesday Market in Newport, where he could rub shoulders with the Island's farmers—every one of whom he knew by name—and drink a few pints with them at the Wheatsheaf in St Thomas' Square, his favourite pub.

As a child, however, he was irrepressibly high-spirited. A constant stream of irate parents and neighbours would arrive at the Fox household to complain about Uffa's fighting, trespassing, practical joking and generally riotous behaviour. But Mrs Fox, they soon discovered, would not hear a word against her only son and resolutely defended him against every accusation.

His father, Arthur, was more of a disciplinarian. Uffa would recall, 'Throughout my growing years I was always tickled by

36   HMY *Britannia*, launched in 1893, was the most successful racing yacht of all time. King George V wanted her to be interred upon his death, and so she was—scuttled in St Catherine's Deep in 1936.

my father's attitude towards me. If I did well at school, sports or games, I was his son, but when, as often happened, I did something wrong, he would snort furiously and turning to my mother would say, "that boy of yours!"' Uffa was regularly beaten at school and at home, later claiming that a 'good caning … has nothing but a good effect on a boy. He has done wrong, had his fun, now he has punishment for it. The whole thing is over in a few minutes; there is no mental anguish, but only bodily pain that you can understand and feel.'

This might seem unremarkable; in Edwardian England, corporal punishment was routine in schools, as well as homes and even magistrates' courts, although flogging had been abolished in the army and navy. Uffa's father, however, appears to have gone a little beyond what, even then, was considered normal. To be sure that the welts were visible, and the strokes would always fall in the same place, he caned on the bare buttocks. Uffa would be told to fill a jug with water and bring it upstairs to his parents' bedroom. When the caning was over and Uffa had thanked his father for the punishment, the water would be mixed with whisky and the two would share a convivial drink.[37]

Even Arthur, however, was nonplussed when a letter arrived from the school accusing Uffa of throwing stones at a hen coop and killing one of the chickens. In the days before battery farming, chicken was a luxury reserved for special occasions, and the school demanded payment for the lost bird. Arthur, who was always careful with money, reflected for a day or two before writing back and offering to pay if he was given the dead chicken. He had shrewdly guessed that the bird had long ago been eaten and he heard nothing more.[38]

Uffa taught himself to swim by secretly plunging into a quiet stretch of the Medina. So confident was he, that he immediately swam out of his depth and practised swimming under water at his first attempt. Arthur was also a strong

---

37 Fox, Uffa. *Joys of Life*. Newnes. 1966.
38 Dixon, June, *UFFA FOX: A Personal Biography*, Angus & Robertson, 1978.

swimmer, and he took care to teach Uffa the complicated and fierce tides of the Medina and Solent to be sure he never got into difficulties. They would dive together from increasing heights, including the yardarms of the old square riggers then moored in the Medina. Uffa later kept an upper deadeye from one of those ships, *Valhalla*, as a doorstop in his office, and a reminder of his childhood.[39]

In his autobiography, Uffa recalled, '… on both sides of the river on the mud, were berthed various vessels, schooners, brigs, topsail schooners, brigantines and steam yachts, with such names as *The White Lady, Boadicea, The Maid of Honour, St George, Sunbeam, Oceana*, and many other famous yachts, most of which had seen all the seas of the known world. And hereabouts were the Curnubia Yard, Groves and Gutteridge Yard and John Samuel White's shipyard, famed for its torpedo boats and torpedo-boat destroyers. Immediately below J S White's yard there was a pair of chains spanning the Medina to enable the steam-driven Floating Bridge to cross the river to and fro, every ten minutes, travelling halfway across on steam and the other half on its vacuum.'[40]

Uffa and his friends would take swimming, boxing and wrestling lessons from Bob Savage, the licensee of the Folly Inn. Bob was a gentle giant who had once been the Royal Navy's heavyweight boxing champion. He was a popular and respected figure—liked and trusted by everyone—and undoubtedly one of Uffa's earliest role models. Set on the eastern bank of the Medina River, just below the drying level, the Folly was, and remains, a popular riverside pub. It gained its name from a barge, *La Follie*, which served beer to bargemen during the 1700s.[41] The Folly can only be accessed down a long unadopted road and is rarely discovered by tourists (unless they arrive by boat); hence, the clientele tend to be Islanders. Uffa, and some of the older boys who could

---

39   A deadeye is a wooden block used to tighten lanyards and shrouds.
40   Fox, Uffa. *Joys of Life*. Newnes. 1966.
41   *The Uffa Fox Trail*, East Cowes Heritage Centre, 2022.

already swim, were allowed to cross the Medina to the old Werrar Brickyard, where they would find swallows' eggs in the brick-drying sheds. They tried to carry them back in their mouths but were often rewarded with a gulp of foul-tasting addled yoke. In later years, Uffa would revive the once famous Folly Regatta and today the site boasts a marina.

The Fox family were musical, as were many families in an age when people made their own entertainment. Uffa was taught to play the piano, the violin and the single-stringed Japanese fiddle, with which he performed at Town Hall concerts in Japanese costume. When he was ten, his grandfather arranged for him to join the choir at St James's Church. Lucy loved to hear children sing, and Grandfather John thought it might instil some discipline in an unruly young boy, as the older choirboys had a reputation for being tough on new recruits.

Uffa had a fine treble voice that had already been coached by Dr Rogerson who was, himself, a composer, organist and choirmaster. Uffa sang beautifully and music would become the third passion of his life, along with the sea and the country. One of his colleagues later recalled him as 'a boy chorister with a ferret showing beneath his cassock singing in a very high key as though all the devils in hell were after him.'[42] For the rest of his days, he would especially enjoy the sound of children singing, stopping his horse when he heard it and singing himself whenever the mood took him. In his later years, Uffa and Prince Philip would lead the singing at the Royal London Yacht Club's Cowes Week dinner.

The other choirboys, as predicted, subjected Uffa to a series of tough initiation tests, including throwing him into a pond. He survived them all, but not with the outcome that Grandfather John had hoped for. Once accepted, Uffa became a willing participant and, ultimately, the ringleader of the mischief they constantly played on one another and the citizens of East Cowes. Uffa had easily passed an audition

42   Dixon, June, *UFFA FOX: A Personal Biography*, Angus & Robertson, 1978.

Uffa joined the choir of St James's Church in East Cowes at the age of ten. Image courtesy of Mike Dixon.

with the choirmaster, Ronald Jackman, but, following his first choir practice, the other boys followed him into the unlit streets before seizing him and dragging him into the pitch-dark graveyard. There they pushed aside a lose headstone and thrust Uffa deep into a tomb. Fortunately for him, he remained silent, despite suffering from mild claustrophobia. If he had cried out, he would have been held captive until the screams had stopped.

The dark evenings after choir practice provided many opportunities for tomfoolery. The boys especially disliked one young man who, they knew, walked down York Avenue every evening on his way to meet his fiancée. They placed an enticing parcel on the pavement with a string attached to it. Each time the victim bent down to pick it up, the boys pulled the box out of his grasp. This went on for several nights until the victim had clearly begun to lose his patience. Finally, they left the box just within his reach, guessing that he would take a running kick at it from sheer frustration. He did so, and his toes struck a gift-wrapped brick which had been soaked in water to make it doubly heavy. His shout of pain had the boys laughing so much he almost caught up with them, but they had placed a tripwire across the passageway that sent him sprawling across the pavement. Bleeding and with his clothes torn, a chase followed through the streets and gardens of East Cowes, but the boys knew those streets better than he did, and he never caught up with them. Uffa and three of the other choirboys would remain friends for life and were still in contact as they approached their seventies.

Uffa had been taught to handle rifles and guns from an early age. His father had a rifle range in the garden, with targets at twenty-five, fifty and one hundred yards. Arthur was an expert shot, especially with a .22 rifle, and he kept a collection of guns and rifles in their cases next to his billiard cues. Uffa, in turn, became an accomplished marksman and developed an early fascination with fire and explosions, especially fireworks. One Guy Fawkes Night, he and his friends lit the fuse of a giant Roman candle and left it smouldering on an iron seat below a gas lamp in York Avenue. As they did so, they saw the shiny buttons of a policeman emerging from the fog. They ran to a nearby gate from where they could observe, and saw the constable grasp the firework, which immediately exploded and burned his hand. Uffa was so doubled up with laughter that he could not run away, and the policeman caught up with him, put him across his knee and gave him a sound thrashing with his belt.

Uffa would always delight in practical jokes, especially those involving explosions. In the 1950s, he and Max Aitken, having enjoyed a very good dinner at the Royal London Yacht Club, decided to fire the Club's prized Trafalgar Cannon, which had been with Nelson at Santa Cruz. The brass gun had not been used for more than a century but, undeterred, they charged it with the powder they'd removed from some starting gun cartridges, stuffed the barrel with damp newspaper, and put a match to the touch hole. There was a tremendous flash and an explosion which could be heard several miles away. The percussion broke some of the Club's windows, and a passing ship was so alarmed that they radioed to shore and notified the police. Two constables soon arrived but were placated by Uffa and Max, who ushered them inside and offered them the hospitality of the Club.[43]

Japes aside, Uffa never lost his love for church and classical music. Wherever he lived there was a Steinway piano, perfectly tuned, and he always eschewed twentieth-century jazz, pop, and rock music, dismissing them as 'the miserable whining songs of the young … music can paint wonderful pictures for those who can listen, love and understand and it can be one of the most inspiring things in the whole of the wide world. The language of music is international and it speaks directly to the heart, its influence is boundless.'[44]

43   Letter to RLYC from former Commodore, R L Bradbeer, ND.
44   Fox, Uffa. *Joys of Life*. Newnes. 1966.

Another great influence on the young Uffa was the Sea Scouts. In 1912, Warrington Baden-Powell—the brother of Scout Movement founder Robert Baden-Powell—had created a special division of the Boy Scouts with its own identity and uniform dedicated to boating and water-based activities. Harry and Eric White of the J S White shipyard formed a Cowes division and Uffa was an early recruit. Harold Lidstone, who had been the Chief Designer at Thorneycroft, tested the boys' proficiency in a host of disciplines and Uffa quickly gained a chest full of badges—he already knew how to swim and row, had learned most of the knots, and his father had taught him the complicated tidal patterns of the Solent.[45] Lidstone also lent them his ten-foot rowing and sailing dinghy. At the same time a member of the Royal Yacht Squadron donated £100 to buy a gig and a seven-ton cutter. An old yacht store in East Cowes, loaned by the boatbuilder George Marvin & Son, became the Sea Scouts' clubhouse. Uffa quickly rose through the ranks, first to King's Scout, then to Assistant Scout Master and, finally, to Scout Master.

---

45   Girls were not admitted to all sections of the Scouts until 1991.

Chapter 3
Valhalla

The boys quickly became proficient, confident sailors and oarsmen. There are few better training grounds than the Solent, with its unique combination of fierce tides and currents, changeable weather, large commercial and military ships, wrecks, shoals, spits, submerged rocks, and practically every other challenge to be found in British coastal waters. Before long, they were allowed to sail beyond Cowes harbour and make longer journeys around the Solent. At lunchtime on a Saturday, they would arrive at the clubhouse with food for the weekend. The first night would often be spent camped overnight on the beach at Colwell Bay, from where they would take mail and food to the lighthouse keepers at the Needles. They thought little of rowing long distances: to Lee-on-Solent for ice creams—a twelve-mile journey across the tide—or to Colwell Bay just for lemonade: this was a twenty-four-mile round trip, but anticipating the tide would cut the distance down to twenty. It often took two of them, using dustpans, to bail out the constant spray. They challenged other crews to a rowing race around the Island, but there were no takers.

They were well trained but, for all their skill, they sometimes took risks that would have terrified their parents if they had known. On one trip they came ashore on the

Dorset coast, west of Anvil Point, against rocks which were 'as hard as hammered iron'. A high-breaking sea was rising and falling by up to eight feet and few other sailors would have risked landing there. Uffa, however, dropped anchor in the comparatively calm waters of St Albans Race, and then, with all sails lowered and the boys rowing 'opposite thwarts', he steered the boat stern first using an oar over the transom, veering away the anchor warp until they were dropping up and down just inches from the rocks. The boys then took it in turns to jump ashore and run the fifty feet to safety, timing their leap with the rise and fall of the boat. Uffa's account of their adventure was a masterpiece of understatement: 'All that was needed for success was perfect timing and a calm heart.'[46]

Their favourite vessel was the whaleboat that had hung from the davits of *Valhalla*, the old square-rigged steam yacht belonging to George Marvin & Son, which lay moored in the Medina River. *Valhalla*'s whaleboat had been designed to take the harpooneer, his crew and a thousand pounds of gear from the mother ship in pursuit of a pod— potentially a distance of many miles—and then safely return with a whale of up to eighty tonnes in tow. Consequently, she was highly seaworthy and rugged but, at the same time, surprisingly light for a boat that was thirty-two feet and six inches at the waterline. She displaced just 750 pounds, so she could easily be hauled up a beach and they could land on shores other boats could not approach. The Sea Scouts loved her, trusted her and were never let down by her. Uffa's special affection for whaleboats may, in part, have been influenced by his famous great-grandfather who had been a harpooneer. He would later recall, 'She was swift and seaworthy, climbing the waves as easily and gracefully as an ocean bird, and those who have not sailed in a lightly built whaleboat have missed one of the greatest joys of sailing. Such a boat fills one with the buoyant hope that springy turf

---

46   Fox, Uffa, *Joys of Life*, Newnes. 1966.

imparts on a sunny day. We sailed her summer and winter for years, and she filled us with the confidence of a trusted friend, as she should, for the whaleboat is the finest sea boat ever evolved by man.'[47] Uffa would, in time, become a master of fast, lightly built sailing boats.

In the Sea Scouts, Uffa quickly evolved into a natural leader. The other boys respected him and mostly accepted his authority, knowing that it was tempered with humour and friendship. They also discovered, however, that he had a fierce temper, and his rages could be extreme. When a fellow Sea Scout, Spot Smith, pinned up a caricature of him in the clubhouse, he flew into such a frenzy that he shattered a window with an iron bar, prompting the other boys to smash everything in sight.

Sailing began to occupy every evening and weekend of Uffa's spare hours. At the same time, although he had a quick mind and an excellent memory, his school results were poor. He was easily distracted and only applied himself to the subjects that really interested him. At the age of fourteen, he failed the scholarship examination which would have allowed him to continue in full-time education.

Had Uffa concentrated a little more, he would, most likely, have gone on to qualify as a naval architect. He was a highly numerate and naturally gifted engineer who would probably have joined a major shipbuilder at a time when Britain's merchant and naval fleets were the largest in the world and her shipyards built three-quarters of the world's tonnage. In Edwardian England, however, boys of his background who failed to win scholarships were guided towards apprenticeships, rather than academe. He joined the local engineering company, S E Saunders, as an apprentice boatbuilder. This turned out to be a remarkable stroke of fortune which played a key part in his later success.

Sam Saunders had begun building steam and petrol-

---

47   Fox, Uffa, *Joys of Life*, Newnes, 1966.

powered launches on the River Thames at Goring in the late nineteenth century (his family owned the famous Swan Inn at Streatley). Reliable waterproof adhesives had yet to be developed, and he invented 'Consuta', a novel way of constructing watertight hulls by using copper wire to sew together mahogany panels which had first been interleaved with calico. It was a winner, and his business began to grow. He also designed and built one of the first sidewall air-cushion craft. This was not a complete success, but his other fast launches were popular. By the early twentieth century, he had seen that Cowes, with royal patronage, was becoming an increasingly popular yachting centre, and he moved his business first to Birmingham Road and later to Columbine Road in East Cowes. By now, he had acquired the British rights to an ingenious system that fed air aft of multi-stepped hulls, thereby reducing friction and increasing the speed. He was soon building hydroplanes to his own patented designs and by 1910 his *Columbine* had won fourteen national motorboat races at speeds of over 30 knots.[48]

The shape of hydroplanes allows hydrodynamic forces to lift their hulls and reduce the wetted area. No longer supported by buoyancy alone, the reduction in friction makes planing hulls hugely faster than traditional designs. A more advanced Saunders powerboat, *Maple Leaf IV*, could reach the previously undreamt of speed of 50 knots on water, and in 1912 had regained the Harmsworth Cup from America. By then, Saunders had seen the potential for designing flying boats with hulls that planed—a crucial development that would help them overcome the suction created as they took off. Tommy Sopwith, who would later become the most successful aircraft designer of World War One, persuaded Saunders to build a lightweight planing hull for his 'Bat Boat', a two-man biplane flying boat. It was a success and was used extensively by the Royal Naval Air Service (RNAS). From

48   Taylor, J W R, *A Short History of Saunders-Roe*, 1960.

Maple Leaf IV was the first boat in the world to attain a
speed of 50 knots.

this moment, Sam Saunders saw his future in flying boats and
by 1915 his company had ceased all other production (the
only exception being RNLI lifeboats). S E Saunders (later
Saunders-Roe) would, in time, become a major manufacturer
of flying boats and, ultimately, hovercraft.

Working hours for apprentices were long: from six o'clock
in the morning until five o'clock in the evening (with breaks
for breakfast and lunch) and on Saturday morning until
noon. Choir practice, which had been three evenings per
week with two services on Sunday, was dropped but his
passion for the Sea Scouts continued. There were regular
evening rowing excursions and longer journeys around the
Solent at weekends. The advent of the First World War saw
S E Saunders receiving large government contracts. Uffa
adapted well to the work, but he had exacting standards and
did not hesitate to criticise older and more experienced men
if he thought he saw a fault in their labour. Like his father and
grandfather before him, he was a perfectionist who would

complain of the smallest flaw, and this did not always endear him to his colleagues.

Uffa began work in the Seaholme shop under Fred Goatley, producing hydroplanes, flying boats and twenty-one-foot racing motorboats. Fred would later achieve fame as the designer of the legendary cockleshell canoes of World War Two. The Chief Designer was then S E Porter, a kindly but exacting boss who allowed the boys to call him 'Joe'. The craftsmanship and skill that went into all of these vessels was outstanding, as were the materials they used, and Uffa's natural perfectionism was further ingrained. He later described his colleagues as 'the finest set of craftsmen I've ever seen.'[49] One of them, Billie Bint, became a lifelong friend and when, later in life, he looked after the rowing fleet at Radley College, on the River Thames, Uffa liked to visit him there and talk about old times. His long-term ambition remained, however, to become a naval architect, and he enrolled in evening classes under Archer Brading, the Chief Draughtsman of the J S White shipyard. Brading would quickly recognise that Uffa was an exceptional pupil. Many years later he would say, 'His quest for knowledge was unlimited, and he was very quick to grasp all that was told him. His big asset is his wonderfully retentive memory.'[50]

As a master carpenter, Arthur Fox kept a well-equipped woodworking shop in a shed at the bottom of his garden. When Uffa asked his father to lend him enough money to buy the materials needed to construct a boat, Arthur simply pointed to a nearby oak and said, 'provided you properly grub out the roots and only cut it in the dead of winter, when there is little sap, you can take what you need from that tree.' Uffa did so and managed to cut both the keel and stem in such a way that the shape he needed was naturally embedded in the wood, without having to steam or bend the timber into

---

49   Fox, Uffa, *Joys of Life*, Newnes, 1966.
50   Speech given at the launch of the Uffa Fox–designed yacht, *Wishbone*. 1935

shape. He would continue to use and perfect this technique throughout his long career as a boatbuilder. Years later, he and Bill Waight, his chief draughtsman, would travel the length and breadth of the Isle of Wight looking for oak and elm trees with the right shape. When they found one, they would buy it from the farmer (Uffa knew them all) and fell it themselves on the coldest day of winter, often camping in the woods for several days. Once down, Bill would lay his templates across the trunk and boughs to be certain that he could cut the components he needed as single, naturally shaped sections. This expensive and laborious method was one of the reasons that Uffa lost money on most of the boats that he sold, but it was also one of the reasons that he earned a reputation for incomparable quality. The Olympic sailor and naturalist, Sir Peter Scott, would liken Uffa's boats to violins, so exquisitely were they built.

That first boat was never completed and Uffa's beautifully shaped keel was, eventually, sawn into gateposts by his father. His next project, however, was more fruitful. S E Saunders sold him their first hydroplane on condition that it was broken up and never used as a powerboat. He and his father converted the hull into a sixteen-foot sailing canoe especially adapted for cruising. It was Uffa's first successful boat, and it set his life on a course from which he would never deviate.

Global events, however, were about to intervene. Because of the military contracts awarded to S E Saunders during World War One, their artisans and apprentices were considered to be in a 'reserved occupation' and were exempt from military service. In spite of this, Uffa was called up into the RNAS. It may simply have been an administrative error, or S E Saunders may have willingly rid themselves of a rebellious spirit but, whatever the reason, Uffa was enlisted 'like a shot out of a gun.' While it may have helped to form his character, it would not be an entirely happy experience. Uffa was too much of an extrovert and free spirit to take easily to military discipline and rules.

His applications to be trained as a pilot were ignored and he would spend much of the war repairing and maintaining the same flying boats he had once helped to build. After initial training at Blandford, he was posted to the seaplane base at South Denes, Great Yarmouth. Further disappointment followed when he failed to make the first teams in cricket or football, but he won a medal at cross-country running. In April 1918, the RNAS was merged with the Royal Flying Corps to create the Royal Air Force.

Following the Armistice, Uffa was finally demobbed, but that too was a painful process. Such was his reputation that a sergeant personally accompanied him to the railway station to make sure he boarded the train back to Blandford. Once there, he was housed in an insanitary and crowded bell tent while waiting for his final discharge. The tents let in the snow, men became ill and some even died of pneumonia. Uffa believed he only avoided illness by sleeping with his pyjamas over his clothes and then washing and drying each garment every day. When his discharge papers finally came through, he found he had been classified as a coal miner and he remained on the reserve list for the next fifty years!

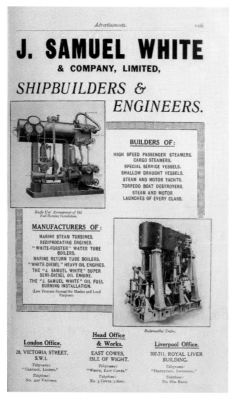

Chapter 4
Typhoon

Disillusioned, but seasoned by an experience that he considered a waste of time, the twenty-year-old Uffa returned to East Cowes to find that his family had moved to a new, larger house in Mayfield Avenue. His father had come up in the world and Uffa's nephew, Tony Dixon, would later recall, 'He [Arthur Fox] was a rate collector for one of the councils. Of course, in those days, the councils were all split up into different areas and I think he was the East Cowes collector. But he was a lovely old chap and used to teach me to play crib. He lived in the house opposite us, the other side of the road, called "Barona" and he actually owned all the houses … and he owned a couple down, further down, in East Cowes. So, we, sort of were reasonably comfortable.'[51]

Comfortable or not, Arthur was always careful with money and he and Lucy still supplemented their income by taking in lodgers, usually instructors from the nearby naval college. The carpentry workshop was not lost either: the old shed from Osborne Road had been carefully dismantled and reassembled—in a slightly larger form—in the new garden.

Uffa returned to S E Saunders to finish his apprenticeship, completing the final six months at the Thames Ironworks in London. There he worked on the great ships of the British India Steam Navigation Company, at the time one of the

51   Kerley, Lisa, *Memories of the Sea—Interview with Tony Dixon*, 29th August 2018.

largest merchant fleets in the world. He remained, as before, an argumentative and critical employee who continually tried the patience of the foremen and senior craftsmen. It came as a relief to some of them when his seven-year term finally ended, and he moved on. This began an unsettled period of his life where he drifted in and out of jobs. He returned to Cowes with a girlfriend, Margaret, in tow, but Lucy found her London ways too forward for either Island life or the family's taste, and she soon went home.

Uffa loved to be at sea and rarely turned down any chance to join a crew, despite suffering badly from seasickness. The Isle of Wight usually protects the Solent from the worst storms but, when wind is against tide, it can be rough. On virtually every voyage, even on large vessels, he would be sick for at least the first seven days before regaining his sea legs. Bill Nutting, with whom Uffa would sail the Atlantic, said he was the only man he knew who could sing when seasick![52]

In 1920, the thirty-five-foot ketch *Typhoon* navigated the Atlantic non-stop from Nova Scotia to Cowes. Such a crossing would be routine today but, at the time, it was an unusual journey for such a small boat, and it aroused a lot of interest, especially as two of the crew were journalists who planned to cover the Cowes Regatta of that year. When *Typhoon* arrived in record time, despite departing two and a half weeks later than planned, many were impressed but the *New York Tribune* wrote a disapproving editorial: 'This sort of cruising is too dangerous to be considered sensible yachting and hardly the sort of thing for American yachtsmen to emulate.' *Typhoon,* having been specially built for the crossing, was new and could easily have been sold in Cowes, but her skipper was determined to sail her back. When Uffa heard that they were short of two crew for the return voyage he, along with his friend Charley Hookey (then only eighteen), volunteered.

---

52   Nutting, William Washburn, *The Track of the Typhoon*, Motor Boat Publishing, New York, 1922.

Typhoon

In 1920, William Atkin designed *Typhoon* for Bill Nutting of *Motor Boat* magazine.

The owner/skipper, Bill Nutting, had seen the boys manoeuvring their whaleboat on the previous day and he welcomed them aboard: 'That evening the solution came in the form of a boatload of Sea Scouts. I had seen and admired these youngsters in the Hamble River the day before, and as they luffed their long rakish whaleboat alongside *Typhoon* with all the snap and skill of an American Coastguard crew, I had an idea. They too had had one, for it seems that there were all sorts of stories afloat about the plans of the *Typhoon*. They clambered aboard and their interest in every last detail of our equipment, and their keen intelligence, was most refreshing. Fox, the scoutmaster, a stalwart youth of twenty-three, explained that he had tried to bring up his nippers in the way that they should go, and they certainly did reflect a lot of good hard training. They all wore the characteristic British Sea Scout uniform, jersey and shorts with bare legs. Fox explained, without further formality, that he would like to go back with us and that if we needed another hand, Hookey, one of his boys, a youngster of eighteen, with an overall length of six feet two inches, would like to go too, or rather, he felt that they would be able to do it, for there wasn't one of all the boatload who was not itching to sign on.'[53] Uffa's father, however, was less enthusiastic.

Bill Nutting and Jim Dorset were journalists on the American magazine *Motor Boat* and, not surprisingly, had more experience under power than under sail. Arthur Fox, who had been a boatbuilder himself, had seen *Typhoon* and did not think she was up to the return journey, which would be on a southerly route with a greater risk of equinoctial storms. In his view, she was too much like a motorboat. Uffa recalled the conversation: 'I said that she had already crossed the Atlantic, and he was not impressed, for he said, "If you threw a box overboard in North America it would cross the Atlantic and be unable to help itself coming to England"; and he warmed up to September gales, and the storms of October and November, from which I gathered he was against my starting.'

He was largely right and Uffa himself would later write, 'When looking at *Typhoon's* lines they do not appear so unbalanced. The easy hollow bow and the powerful stern are typical of motorboats, which tend to squat by the stern through the propeller kicking away the ground, or rather the water, from under their quarters. *Typhoon's* lines, every time I look at them, bring to my eyes a picture of two sailing men, lovers of sail, made through force of circumstances prisoners in the offices of a Motor Boat Journal, and while there, being unable to stifle their love of sail any longer, they break out with a sailing boat, which to appear in their paper must bear a strong resemblance to a motor boat.'[54]

All of the Sea Scouts and a small group of friends gathered to see them off and they began what was, at first, a pleasant cruise along the French and Spanish coasts and then west

53   Nutting, William Washburn, *The Track of the Typhoon*, Motor Boat Publishing, New York, 1922.
54   Fox, Uffa, *Sailing, Seamanship and Yacht Construction*, Peter Davies, 1934.

Typhoon

Bill Nutting at the helm of *Typhoon*.

to the Azores. In Ponta Delgada they took on a fifth crew member but were unable to properly provision the boat. Between 1920 and 1921 the Azores and Cape Verde Islands suffered a drought so severe that it led to a famine. There was a chronic food shortage accompanied by an outbreak of bubonic plague, and soldiers were guarding the quays to prevent any visiting ship from loading edible stores. On 19 October *Typhoon* set sail with the bare minimum of food needed for the long journey to New York. By early November they encountered heavy Atlantic storms and by now were reduced to eating small pancakes made from flour and water: the only provisions left on board. Even those had to be cooked on a Primus as the weather made it impossible to use the stove. By 13 November the wind was so strong they could only fly one small trysail. By 17 November conditions were even worse and they trailed two thick warps over the stern, one with a bucket attached, to try and stabilise the boat. Water was now pouring into the cockpit, and on one occasion she heeled so badly that the masts actually touched the water before she righted herself.

They hove-to and tried to deploy a sea anchor but, as they did so, they were hit by another massive wave which fully capsized them. Uffa recalled, 'That sea towered above us like a church; in moments like that size cannot be judged accurately, for the brain is too excited, but to me it looked to have a face that was practically vertical, but with the top overhanging, like an overhanging cliff, and the top seemed to be thirty feet above us, and we had already climbed about fifteen feet from its base. So there *Typhoon* seemed to me to be climbing the face of a plumb cliff, and when she had climbed fifteen feet the other thirty feet crashed down on her.' [55] This time the masts hit the water and continued for another twenty degrees.

Jim Dorset was swept overboard but, miraculously, managed to catch one of the trailing warps and hold on to it. Uffa also went overboard, but the mast came down on top of him and he was able to cling to the hounds, which were three-quarters of the way up. As the boat righted herself, he slid down the mast to the deck, breaking his toe, but still able to release the small, solitary trysail which slowed the boat enough to haul in Jim, still clinging to the warp. They got him to the counter, but he no longer had the strength to hold on and kept sliding back down the warp. Uffa grasped his oilskins and wrapped them round a cleat on deck which nearly choked Jim, but Bill Nutting managed to get a boat hook under him and then, prising it down over the rail, got enough leverage to slide him back onboard. The next day Jim wrote in the log: 'I would like to say right here that I owe my life to the cool headedness and quick work of my friends.'

They were alive and although the boat was damaged it remained serviceable. They had no food, however, and still faced a long journey. Reasoning that the remaining food

---

55   Fox, Uffa, *Sailing, Seamanship and Yacht Construction,* Peter Davies, 1934.

would have been wasted if they had died, they ate the last of their emergency rations: a tin of soup, a tin of beef and a tin of vegetables. They even found a bottle of cognac to wash down the meagre meal and slept well that night. The next day the seas eased a little and an exhausted seabird landed on the deck, rested for an hour and then flew off. They were two hundred miles south-east of New York, sailing into a north-westerly wind.

The seas were calmer but still formidable and they had to endure freezing nights with no food. At eleven am on 20 November, they sighted a ship a quarter of a mile away on their starboard bow. Uffa sent a message in semaphore: 'Please report *Typhoon* of New York thirty-one days from the Azores.' The crew of the Spanish ship, SS *Guillem Sorolla*, spoke no English and could not understand the message, but they hove-to anyway, allowing *Typhoon* to come alongside. As soon as they realised, from sign language, that *Typhoon*'s crew were starving, a cornucopia of provisions rained down onto *Typhoon*'s decks: a leg of mutton, a side of beef, sugar, lard, fruit, salmon, and two bottles of cognac. Uffa recalled, 'The captain was quite delighted at having saved us from hunger; when we let go our warps and fell away from the steamer, giving three cheers for her, her captain and crew, and salutes on our foghorn, her powerful steam whistle responded with a succession of deafening blasts.'[56]

Tragically, the *Guillem Sorolla* and her crew were later lost. In October 1922, while carrying coal from Cardiff to Barcelona, she lost power and sank during a storm. The ships that answered her distress calls found no trace of either the vessel or her crew. Years later, the French Hydrographic Service located her wreck on the seabed, and it is still shown on charts. By 1924, Bill Nutting would also have died at sea during another attempt at an Atlantic crossing.

---

56   Fox, Uffa, *Sailing, Seamanship and Yacht Construction,* Peter Davies, 1934.

When the captain of the *Guillem Sorolla* realised that the crew of *Typhoon* was starving, he showered them with provisions.

He and two companions had successfully sailed the forty-two-foot Norwegian fishing-boat-style vessel *Leif Eriksson* from Norway to Iceland, but they subsequently disappeared without trace off the coast of Greenland.[57]

When Uffa finally arrived in New York, he had little money and found great difficulty in working his passage home. At the time, there were more than 2,000 unemployed seamen in the city, all competing for what little work was available. Charley Hookey was fortunate to get a berth as a trimmer on RMS *Celtic*, a luxurious 'Big Four' liner of the White Star Line which sailed from New York to Liverpool. Trimmers shovelled coal until it was level and the ship was safely balanced. It was back-breaking work in dark and dirty conditions, but at least he was going home on a fast, first-class ship. It would be months before Uffa was taken aboard the *Roman Prince* as third cook, which meant, in reality, being the dishwasher, galley cleaner and vegetable peeler. He soon fell out with the skipper and

---

57   Posted in *Adventurous Use of the Sea*: The Cruising Club of America, February 18, 2015.

was put ashore before the ship had sailed. A shoreside job as a longshoreman ended when he got into a bloody fight with the Dutch foreman. He came close to suicide before finally getting a passage home as a deckhand on the SS *Vauban*, a steamer and former troopship of the Lamport and Holt Line, bound for Liverpool. His wretched experience in New York confirmed the low opinion of cities that he would maintain for life.

The whole journey, however, had been a baptism of fire for Uffa. He had fulfilled his long-held dream of making a crossing under sail and visiting the New World. He had survived starvation as well as a terrifying storm and helped save the life of a fellow crew member. He had also, on the long voyage, had time to study the many ways in which a sailing vessel reacts to constantly changing weather. In his book, *Sailing, Seamanship and Yacht Construction*, he would list *Typhoon* first among the many sailing vessels he had known: 'Seamen are made up of deepwater men and coasters, and until I met *Typhoon* and her owner I was a coaster only, not having sailed off soundings.[58] So *Typhoon*, having given me perspective, which, like humour in life, gives a sense of proportion and balance, *Typhoon* shall have the honour of going in to bat first.' [59]

He put the capsize down to a starving crew driving their boat too hard before a gale, and he would record three lessons that he had learned from her:

1. That a small vessel going to windward could stand far more than her crew, but that chasing away before a gale, the crew could drive her beyond her limitations.
2. That one man could reef or stow a 500 ft^2 mainsail in all weathers, but not a larger sail.

---

58   Sailing offshore beyond the 100 fathom line.
59   Fox, Uffa, *Sailing, Seamanship and Yacht Construction*, Peter Davies, 1934.

49

3. That as small vessels can and do capsize, inside
ballast is a source of danger, and if carried should
be fastened down.

Uffa had never left the Sea Scouts and continued to sail
with them whenever he returned to Cowes. On reaching the
age of twenty-one he had been appointed the Scoutmaster
and given responsibility for the other boys. His close friend,
Bill Waight, was the Assistant Scout Master. One of his duties
was to organise and lead short sailing expeditions across the
Solent, sometimes venturing as far as Poole or Weymouth.
Uffa, however, having already crossed the Atlantic, yearned
to sail farther and he began to hatch a plan with his fellow
scouts, all of whom he swore to secrecy. They would take
their whaleboat to France and sail down the Seine to Paris,
but the boys' parents would be told only that they were going
to Poole.

Throughout his life, Uffa inspired others to help him do
remarkable things that were challenging, but not always
wise. He never suffered from a moment's self-doubt and had
astonishing powers of persuasion; once an idea took hold,
nothing could extinguish it. He demanded, and often got,
unwavering allegiance and many of the Sea Scouts would
remain loyal to him for decades, if not for life. Uffa later
recalled, 'We knew our boat inside and out, we were expert
at rowing, sailing, and handling her in all conditions of wind
and sea, but above all this I had from every boy INSTANT
OBEDIENCE.'[60] Each of them would have understood the
risks of crossing the English Channel in a small open boat,
but none of them doubted either the ruggedness of their
whaleboat or Uffa's helmsmanship.

In addition to Bill Waight and himself, Uffa took eight
boys aged from fourteen to eighteen. Knowing that weight
would be a problem, they carried the bare minimum of water,

60   Fox, Uffa, *Joys of Life*, Newnes, 1966.

clothing and provisions for a voyage of a hundred miles. Uffa was always eccentric and one of his many peculiarities was a conviction that shoes and socks were unnecessary, so he forbade them. Water was so strictly rationed that each boy was allowed only six sucks from a beaker per day.

As usual, they camped for the first night in Colwell Bay and sailed the following morning. Uffa wrote in the log: 'We left Colwell Bay. Conway, the Coxswain of Totland Bay Lifeboat reckons we will be back in an hour or so as there is still a lump on outside the Needles left over from the last three days southwest blow. Told him to put his head in a bag!' They rounded the Needles, sailing their whaleboat into a strong sou'wester with a dipping lug.[61] The glass was falling and there were spots of rain, hardly a good omen, but Uffa described his crew as, 'a little awed but determined.' There was so much spray that two of the crew had to bail constantly but, by sunset the wind had calmed, and they began to row. Uffa slept during the day but asked to be woken at dusk because, 'at sunset the Lord tells those who understand what the night will be,' and he always took the helm at night. He recalled, 'It was wonderful to watch the sky turn to red with yellow and silver clouds, and then to see all the colours turning gradually to a deep blue that was almost as black as darkness spread across the surface of the sea.' [62] The mainsail was never reefed or lowered because Uffa always had a trusted scout on the mainsheet who could release it in a second.

The boys took turns to sleep, as best they could, across the thwarts but, before long, they were shouting from the pain of cramp. Several of them, including Uffa, were seasick but otherwise they were in good spirits, and soon found themselves sailing gently across a calm sea under a blue sky. At dawn, following their second night at sea, they sighted Cap de la Hève with Le Havre in its shadow. Once safely berthed

---

61   A boomless sail whose yard is lowered or 'dipped' when tacking to bring the sail around to the leeward side of the mast.
62   Fox, Uffa, *Joys of Life*, Newnes, 1966.

LEAVING COWES, A CLOSE UP OF "ROWLOCK TOES"
"ROWING OUT OF COWES" ② XX

"ANXIOUS" SKIPPER STEERS
ALL NIGHT
AFTER STEERING ALL NIGHT ④ XX

Una kept a diary and photographed each step of the Sea Scouts' attempt to reach Paris. These images, captioned by Uffa, come from his personal album — courtesy of Mike Dixon.

WE SIT AFT SO THE WHALER WILL NOT SHEER ABOUT AS THE SWALLOW ~~DOES~~ GETS ALONG AT 8 KNOTS.

3½

WE WANDER TO THE SEA FRONT AND ~~HAVE~~ A HAVRE

⑤ xx

in the harbour, they toured the town and played football on the beach. It would be a short visit, however, for that evening they entered the Seine via the Tancarville Canal and began to sail and row towards Rouen on the flood tide, reaching La Roque in two hours.

They spent a day in Rouen, and then continued up the non-tidal Seine as far as Meulan, only thirty miles from Paris. Here, Uffa finally had to accept that they no longer had time to reach Paris, and he reluctantly turned for home. A friendly steamer, the *Swallow* from Grimsby, towed them back as far as the Le Havre roads from where a south-westerly wind bore them back to the Isle of White. Although still many miles from home, in the night sky they could see the powerful lighthouse of St Catherine's reflected in the clouds, long before they saw the coast. They made landfall at Ventnor, but the tides were not favourable for a return to Cowes by either the western or eastern route. Two of the boys, Spike Crews and Spot Smith, had to be at work the following morning, so they walked barefoot through the night from Ventnor to East Cowes, a distance of fifteen miles. Uffa counted the adventure as a great success and wrote of it fondly in his autobiography, making no mention of the parents' fury over the unauthorised journey. For two weeks no one had known where the boys were, or even if they were still alive. The entire committee of the Cowes Sea Scouts resigned in protest, accusing Uffa of putting the boys' lives at risk, and Uffa was dismissed as Scoutmaster.

HOMEWARD BOUND. WE TURNED BACK AT MEULAN. AS TIME WOULD NOT ALLOW US TO GO TO PARIS. WE LET GO THIS FLEET OF BARGES AND GET IN TOW OF A FASTER LOT.

Chapter 5
Radiant

I f Uffa's spirits were dampened by his expulsion from the Sea Scouts, it was not for long. He was now firm in his ambition to become an independent designer and builder of boats, and he asked his father to lend him the money to get him started. In the meantime, he wrote to practically every other boatbuilder in Cowes, looking for work. The letters were long, rambling and far removed from any normal job application. George Marvin & Son were so intrigued that they kept their letter for posterity. Uffa signed off with the postscript: 'Well, I hope I have not given you the guts ache by blowing my own trumpet so much, but if I don't who will, and I want a job in your yard if there is a chance.' And then, for no obvious reason, he added his personal views on women: 'A faint heart never won a fat woman. You know there are only two kinds of women, thin and fat, and the fat are the better of the two. It is all very well for people to say the nearer the bone the sweeter the meat, but dammit there is very little meat on a thin woman to be sweet. And their legs are like canaries.' The company treasured the letter but did not offer him a job.

There was an election for the local council and Uffa, now several years past his twenty-first birthday, voted for the first time. One of the candidates had died suddenly, and there had not been time to remove his name from the ballot papers. The late councillor had been a friend of Uffa's family and a visitor to their house. Throughout Uffa's life, he would hold politicians in contempt, and he put his cross next to the man's name, writing beneath it: 'THE ONLY GOOD COUNCILLOR IS A DEAD ONE.' Word quickly spread around East Cowes and Uffa's angry father, who worked for the council and liked to be on good terms with them, confronted him.

'But!' protested Uffa, 'the ballot box is secret. You vote inside a square tent of sackcloth.'

'I know', countered Arthur, 'for I've been voting longer than you have. But first of all, tell me who, except you, of all the people in this town, would think of voting in such a way. And secondly, even if he had, who would dare it?'

Uffa was speechless and, despite his age, his father caned him for the last time. Afterwards they drank a bottle of whisky together and Arthur said, 'As a twig is bent the tree will grow. I've tried to train you so that your fellow men will always enjoy your company. I shall never reprove or punish you again, but while I am on this earth you can always come to me for advice.'

Uffa not only asked his father for advice, but he also asked him for a loan of £5,000 to start his own business, a sum which we must assume Arthur could have afforded. £5,000, adjusted for inflation, comes to roughly £200,000 today, a substantial amount, even for a man who owned a number of properties.[63] Uffa had wisely decided that he would be happier as a small fish in a big pond, rather than the reverse. He eschewed powerboats, aircraft and large sailing boats, deciding instead to concentrate on building small sailing boats that the common man could afford. Within a few years he would become the most successful and influential designer of racing dinghies and small keelboats of his generation or, arguably, of any generation.

Arthur Fox never liked to part with money, but he wanted, all the same, to support Uffa in what he knew had the

---

63   https://www.bankofengland.co.uk/monetary-policy/inflation/inflation-calculator

potential to be a successful business. 'I know your thoughts,' he said, 'but if I give you money, you will only waste it on useless machinery and never realise its full value. So instead of giving you money, I am going to deposit in your bank the deeds of various properties that will come to you on my death. You can overdraw on these up to the amount that the bank will allow but remember that you will have to pay five or six per cent interest, depending on the bank rate, on whatever you overdraw. I will also have a yarn to the timber and other merchants with whom you must deal, so that you can pay them monthly, or whenever you can, as this will save a great deal of trouble for you.'[64] Arthur Fox knew his son well, he had correctly judged that Uffa had a genuine talent for boats and sailing, but he also knew that he spent money too easily and quickly.

Together they took another sound decision: the Fourteen-Foot Class was then growing in popularity. The boats were affordable, fast and fun to sail. A good fourteen-foot design could sell in numbers, whereas a larger yacht might be a one-off. The shed at the bottom of Arthur's garden in Mayfield Avenue was wide enough to accommodate a fourteen-foot hull. Arthur already had most of the necessary tools and there was just enough room to build a second shed for Uffa who could build boats at home until he could afford premises of his own. For extra labour, he could rely on his old Sea Scout friends, several of whom, including Bob Dickerson and Stan (Spike), Crews, would eventually work for him full-time. In the mornings, the floors of the Fox home were often covered with sleeping Sea Scouts. Uffa's mother, however, rarely complained and cheerfully made breakfast for them.

When the boats were ready there was just enough room for the Sea Scouts to turn them on their sides, then carry them past the house and onwards to the Sea Scout hut which was a quarter of a mile away. Bill Waight, the Assistant Scout Master,

---

64   Fox, Uffa. *Joys of Life*. Newnes. 1966.

had passed his school scholarship and qualified as a naval architect, having served an apprenticeship at the J S White Shipyard. In time he would become Uffa's Chief Draughtsman and would not only prepare Uffa's drawings for him but also contribute important ideas to Uffa's most successful boats. But first, Uffa wanted to make another Atlantic crossing, this time aboard the American yacht *Diablesse,* which belonged to friends of Bill Nutting, and Bill was happy to vouch for Uffa's seamanship.

On 17 June 1922, the owner John B Kelley and his wife, along with Uffa, Bill Waight and Bobby Somerset, set sail from Cowes for Madeira en route to New York. At thirty-five tonnes and a length overall of fifty-two feet, the schooner *Diablesse* was a substantially bigger and more stable boat than the ketch *Typhoon.* On this occasion, Arthur Fox was happy with both the design of the boat, and the crew, and raised no objection. Bobby Somerset, the navigator, was heir to a dukedom and a direct descendant of Edward III. He had served in the army, navy and air force during the First World War and won the Distinguished Service Order for exceptional bravery and leadership during the Battle of Cambrai. He had also trained as an RAF pilot, later becoming a noted flyer of autogyros. In the Bermuda Cup Race of 1932, he would save the lives of ten sailors, risking his own life to take them off their burning schooner, *Adriana.* In 1965 he would tragically drown off the coast of Rhodes while, once again, trying to save the lives of others.

In Madeira, they spent four pleasant days, but the water inlet pipe for their engine burst and began to flood the boat. Uffa hit on the idea of loading her bow with heavy stones in order to lift the stern sufficiently to reach the pipe, but it did not work. In the end, a diver had to be called in. Uffa, without breathing apparatus, dived beneath the boat to show him the hole, and was almost drowned when the diver, who had an air supply, held on to him. Decades later, when Uffa appeared on the television programme *This Is Your Life,* Bill Waight

Radiant

At fifty-two feet and thirty-five tonnes, *Diablesse* was significantly bigger than *Typhoon*.

suggested that the diver had deliberately held on because he'd been infuriated by Uffa's constant criticisms. Uffa's grim expression betrayed his feelings about that.

They set sail from Madeira in fair weather, heading south for the trade winds and later turning north for the Saragossa Sea. Uffa recalled: 'We were a little kingdom of our own. The skipper, aged thirty-four, was the father of the family; Bobby and I the elder twins, twenty-four each; and Bill and Miss Ann (as we called the skipper's wife) the younger twins, both being only twenty-one. Day after day passed peacefully by; Bobby reading for an hour every evening out loud to us all in the cockpit, Miss Ann mixing Mint Juleps about 2.00 pm every afternoon, a Virginian drink, which first of all produces smiles, then a great feeling of energy, then a powerful desire for sleep, while, as my trick at the wheel generally started soon after sundown, I used to sing for half an hour with Bill as a helpmate, and Bobby would lead us in *Green grow the Rushes, O*.'[65]

65   Fox, Uffa, *Sailing, Seamanship and Yacht Construction,* Peter Davies, 1934.

In the calm waters of the Saragossa the wind dropped, and they began to bake under the sun. Twenty-eight days later they arrived in Bermuda. To Uffa's delight, the pilot came to meet them in a whaleboat, reminding him and Bill Waight of happy days in the Sea Scouts.

Wherever Uffa came close to shore he always paid close attention to local sailing boats. In Bermuda, they were racing fourteen-footers, a class in which he would later excel. He made this note in his diary: 'On August 10, our sailing day, we watched their fourteen-footers racing. With a thirty-five-foot mast and a sixteen-foot bowsprit they set 350 feet of sail, and the crew of six was hardly enough to sit out this amount of canvas. It was a most interesting race to watch. The dinghies were moored either side of the committee boat, which, as there was no stream, lay head to wind. At the starting gun the dinghies sprang off on either tack; then when they met after coming about, instead of the port tack boat giving way they both went about, the idea being that as the two had done equally well to meet after sailing a certain time neither should have any right of way. There is much to be said for this rule, for there is no doubt that our port rule gives the starboard tack boat a great advantage, equal to about three boats' lengths in practice, and such rules make racing a game of tactics like chess rather than one of pure sailing skill.'[66]

As soon as the race was over, they set sail, using the engine for the first few miles. No one noticed that some oakum had fallen onto the exhaust pipe, and a fire broke out, which quickly became serious. In no time the rear counter was fully ablaze. Uffa was given the job of rowing the pilot back to the harbour. He had to take care because of reefs and sharks, but as soon as the pilot was ashore he turned back, only to find that in the confusion of the fire *Diablesse* had continued to proceed to sea. It was now dark, and the waves had begun

---

66   Fox, Uffa, *Sailing, Seamanship and Yacht Construction*, Peter Davies, 1934.

breaking. Uffa was a strong and experienced oarsman, but it took all of his strength to catch up. He was completely exhausted by the time he came alongside, and the dinghy was taken back onboard.

The boat continued to burn fiercely, and they were forced to smash in the cockpit floor, using the anchor as a battering ram. Uffa, still angry from having been left behind, went into a destructive frenzy, shattering the boards with a will. Once the engine was exposed, they could finally get a hand-pumped hose onto the fire and douse it. With the flames fully out, Uffa used his carpentry skills to rebuild the floor. He noted with pride that his repair remained good twelve years later, and the words: 'Pol Roget Champagne' were still faintly visible under the paint.

They arrived in New York fifty-one days and some 5,000 miles after leaving Cowes. Following two months in Long Island Sound, their long journey ended in Gloucester, Massachusetts, a port that Uffa had always wanted to visit because of the reputation of the Gloucester Schooners. Fortunately for him, the International Fishing Schooner Races were taking place and he could watch *Henry Ford* of America and *Bluenose* of Canada fight for the championship of the North Atlantic. He also ran into old friends, including Bill Nutting and Chris Ratsey, of the famous Cowes-based sailmakers Ratsey & Lapthorn.[67]

It was no longer so difficult to work a passage from New

---

67   Thomas Ratsey (Chris Ratsey's father) joined the family sail-making firm in Cowes at the age of fifteen, and later arranged a merger with the Gosport loft of Lapthorn's. Hugely respected by the entire sailing community (including the king) he lost three sons during World War One. Tom was fond of Uffa and often defended him from criticism. 'Quench not the smoking flax', he would say, whenever someone suggested (as they frequently did) that the young Uffa Fox needed cutting down to size. In Tom's later years, Uffa would often sit with him aboard his much-loved yacht, *Dolly Varden*, listening to his tales. Tom died in 1935 and in 2009 he was inducted into the America's Cup Hall of Fame.

The Gloucester Fishing Schooner *Henry Ford*.

York, and Uffa was able to sign on as a trimmer for a voyage to Antwerp. He became good at it, graduating from trimmer to stoker, and claimed that the satisfaction of placing a shovelful of coal exactly where you intend is akin to the satisfaction a golfer gets from a perfect drive! By New Year of 1923 he was home in Cowes and his mind turned, once more, to the boats he would build and try to sell.

In consultation with his father, and bearing in mind the size of his workshop, he decided his first design would be a

Radiant

fourteen-foot dinghy. 'Fourteening' has a history that goes
back to the origins of racing small open boats at sea. By the
beginning of the twentieth century fourteen-foot, undecked
sailing boats were being raced in many parts of Britain and
abroad, both inland and at sea. In the early years, the designs
and materials used varied greatly from one area to another, but
popular designs included the 'West of England Conference'
dinghies of Teignmouth (originally designed by F W Pengelly),
and the 'Norfolk' dinghies built in Norwich and Kingston-
upon-Thames. By 1911, the designs of the Teignmouth-based
builder Frank Morgan-Giles were gaining popularity and by
the end of the First World War the Yacht Racing Association
(YRA) had broadened its reach by merging with the Boat
Racing Association (BRA) and publishing the first rules for
a National Fourteen class.[68] This brought about an important
change in outlook because, prior to the merger, the YRA had
taken little interest in dinghies. As Sir Peter Scott would later
recall, 'Dinghies were the kind of boat you used to take you to
a larger and more respectable yacht and were not in their own
right regarded as yachts at all.'[69]

Initially, there was little interest, but by 1922 the YRA was
actively promoting the concept of a National Fourteen-Foot
dinghy because of its affordability and capacity to be sailed
both on fresh and salt water.[70] In 1923, the Island Sailing Club
(ISC), based in Cowes, asked Charles Nicholson to design
an open fourteen-foot dinghy with a view to creating an
inexpensive fleet that could race on equal terms. Thirty years
earlier, Nicholson had famously taken just ten days to design
his Redwing, a legendary dinghy for Bembridge Sailing Club,
giving it an especially shallow draft well adapted to their shoal

68   In 1953, at the request of the royal family, the Yacht Racing
Association would become the Royal Yachting Association (RYA).
69   Scott, Peter, *The Eye of the Wind*, Hodder & Stoughton, 1967.
70   https://gbr.international14.org/a-national-
class-1923-1928/

waters.[71] He and his brothers would later form the renowned Camper & Nicholsons boatyard which would design and construct some of the most famous yachts of the twentieth century. Nicholson's fourteen-foot design for ISC was a deep-hulled, clinker-built boat with sloop rig and a short bowsprit that cost around £35 (about £1,700 in today's money), placing it within almost every sailor's means.[72]

Affordability was becoming a contentious issue in dinghy racing. Morgan-Giles' boats were exquisitely made from the finest mahogany, but their price tag—around £100—put them out of reach for all but the wealthiest owners. A 1924 article in *Yachting Monthly* had demanded that 'something needed to be done'. They suggested capping the price of new dinghies, a direct challenge to Morgan-Giles, 'whose skill in designing these boats is well known.'

Frank Morgan-Giles, however, who was in financial straits at the time, responded angrily to the article, hurling brickbats at 'a certain element in the Cowes class', and dismissing the enormous 'sked pieces' and 'towering upper works' which, he felt, characterised their boats. In short, he wanted the Fourteen-Foot class rules (which he'd helped to write) left as they were without any hint of a price cap.[73] He also produced a new design of his own: a carvel-built, U-bowed dinghy which soon proved to be faster than Nicholson's design.[74]

The Cowes sailing community and the Island Sailing Club took offence and fiercely defended their locally designed and built boats. Chris Ratsey wrote to the magazine, accusing Morgan-Giles of having done 'a very gross injustice to the Cowes fourteen-foot dinghy class'. He reminded readers that

71   In 1937 the class was redesigned by Nicholson. The minor changes were used to create the 1938 Redwing that can be seen racing both outside Bembridge Harbour and in Poole Harbour.
72   https://gbr.international14.org/a-national-class-1923-1928/
73   *SEAHORSE* Magazine. ND.
74   https://gbr.international14.org/a-national-class-1923-1928/

Radiant

A 1908 fourteen-foot West of England Conference dinghy designed by Frank Morgan-Giles. Winner of the WEC Cup 1909 & 1910. Under restoration by the Morgan-Giles Heritage Project.

he had come second at Cowes the previous year to 'one of our oldest boats …' He finished with a challenge: Frank Morgan-Giles would always be welcome to race in Cowes, even though 'several boats will be raised up with their "towering upper works" to suit our conditions'. Uffa then upped the ante by offering to race Morgan-Giles for a wager of £5, which Giles promptly increased to £50. The much-postponed race ended with a win for Uffa.

National Fourteens were growing in stature, and this was the ring into which Uffa Fox threw his hat by designing his first racing dinghy, *Ariel*. 'The problem was difficult', Uffa wrote, 'for Giles as a designer was king of the castle and in a very strong position having, in twenty years or more, developed and perfected the Snark type of lines. If I followed, it was obvious that I would always do so, and so I decided to go off on another tack.'[75]

Uffa Fox and Frank Morgan-Giles were polar opposites.

---

75   Fox, Uffa, *Sailing, Seamanship and Yacht Construction*, Peter Davies, 1934.

The Teignmouth designer was censorious, teetotal, reserved, and ordered in everything he did. Uffa had been described by his friend Peter Scott as '... an *enfant terrible*. He had black curly hair, a laugh which stopped all conversation in a crowded room and an irresistible urge to shock the strait-laced.'[76] The two designer/builders would conduct a lengthy and acrimonious public quarrel and never be reconciled. As Uffa put it, 'When a person throws stones it is possible that one of them might hit someone who might be annoyed ...'[77]

Throughout his career Uffa Fox would repeatedly challenge the orthodoxy of yacht and boat building. He was, above all things, an original thinker who took nothing at face value. The fact that a particular design or hull shape might have stood the test of time, was a signal to Uffa that it could be overdue for replacement: 'It was natural that my apprenticeship, served through all this change, taught me to take nothing for granted, nor to accept past designing and construction as unalterable. So, when I started off as a young designer and builder, it was with a mind as free as air; with a restless zest to strive for "newness" in design.'[78] Every shipwright knew that the less wetted surface a hull possesses, the less friction it creates and the faster it will go. Frank Morgan-Giles designed beautiful U-shaped hulls and, as Uffa himself phrased it (in slightly mocking terms) '... that wonderful naval architect was building in his Teignmouth shipyard such perfect examples of the shipwright's art and craft in his wonderful fourteen-footers with these circular sections that it was impossible even to contemplate improving them.'[79] Uffa, in truth, contemplated little else.

During his apprenticeship at S E Saunders, he had worked on many planing hulls, including the record-breaking *Maple Leaf IV*, which had achieved the previously

---

76   Scott, Peter, *The Eye of the Wind*, Hodder & Stoughton, 1967.
77   *SEAHORSE* Magazine. ND.
78   Fox, Uffa, *Sailing Boats*, Newnes, 1959.
79   Fox, Uffa, *Joys of Life*, Newnes, 1966.

---

undreamt of speed of fifty knots on water. He knew that V-shaped hulls have a greater wetted surface when stationary, but they plane much more effectively at speed, and he also knew that there was nothing in the National-Fourteen rules that prohibited V-shaped hulls. He recalled, 'So from the start I set out to design V-section boats that would lift out of the water when sailed hard off the wind, and by halving their displacement sail twice as fast and so be invincible in winds above twelve miles an hour. Below this wind speed, the wind is often far from true so it was possible for any boat to win by a wind shift.'[80]

Although his ambition was unbounded, he was, nevertheless, fairly cautious in his early designs: 'I did not dare to go to the full limit of my ideas at once … for several years I strove to develop a set of hull lines that under sail would hydroplane over water, just as *Maple Leaf IV* did under power. This was against all the then accepted laws of sailing lines, and early on I had nothing but disappointment.'[81]

As he began to employ craftsmen, so he took the precaution of visiting the local trade union official. All of his skilled men belonged to the Shipconstructors' and Shipwrights' Association (SSA), which was later amalgamated into the General Municipal and Boilermakers Society (GMB). He went to the home of their secretary, and told him that he looked upon their union in the same light as he looked upon the Royal Society for the Prevention of Cruelty to Animals (RSPCA): 'I have kept animals all my life without them calling on me to tell me how I should treat them … If you ever come in my works to tell me how to treat men, it would mean that I was not fit to employ them, so I should release them all to the union.'[82] All went well for the first twenty years or so, and Uffa had no problem with the union, but things would change during World War II.

---

80   Fox, Uffa. Joys of Life. Newnes. 1966.
81   Ibid.
82   Ibid.

Cowes-built boats had previously been famous for their 'towering topsides', but a feature of many of Uffa's designs was a noticeable reduction in the amount of freeboard.[83] His carvel hulls were, initially, a halfway house between the U-shaped Morgan-Giles boats and the V sections Uffa would later become famous for. His radical ideas did not only extend to the shape of the hull, however, he also explored new ways of rigging sailing boats, always looking for improvements in speed that were within the rules. He set the mast a full third of the waterline length back from the bow and added a sliding gunter rig, as well as roller reefing gear, which was then unheard of in racing dinghies. In fact, all of his fittings and gear were reduced to the minimum possible weight (Uffa said that weight was only useful in a steamroller!) but not with any loss of strength. His first design, *Ariel*, was launched in 1925 and was still sailing in 1963![84] These features were then considered so radical that he was briefly dubbed 'Madman Fox' and *Ariel* was mocked as a mere 'cockleshell'. The laughter was silenced, however, when he won every race in his class that year! *Ariel* beat the Morgan-Giles boats and all others, although this may have had as much to do with Uffa's skill as a sailor than her inherent speed.

With his future looking more secure he decided it was time to get married. Alma Phillips was the daughter of the miller at the Old East Medina Mill, close to where he'd learnt to swim, and the families had known each other for many years. Alma was a clever, pretty, flaxen-haired girl with the kind of curves that pleased Uffa's eye. He was passionate at the best of times, but in love he was an unstoppable force and he wooed her relentlessly.

They had several things in common: her family were 'river people' who shared the Fox's love of boats and all things

---

83   Freeboard is the distance from the waterline to the upper deck level.
84   https://gbr.international14.org/the-uffa-fox-era-1928-1939

nautical, Alma also enjoyed poetry, music and the arts in general. Uffa begged her to marry him, but she was a practical, down-to-earth schoolteacher, who thought the mercurial young boatbuilder was unstable, hot-headed and unlikely to make a good husband. Alma's father was fond of Uffa, but her mother thought he was too boastful and opinionated for her daughter. Alma turned him down and when he persisted, she accepted a job as head teacher at a girls' school in Dorchester, thinking that would be the end of the matter. Uffa wrote a desperate letter to her, literally threatening suicide if she did not return. His mood swings could be extreme, and she believed his threat. She probably knew that in New York, when he was at rock bottom, he had actually stood on a small swing bridge in Brooklyn, fully intending to throw himself off it. It was only when he tossed his cap aside and the kindly bridge keeper returned it to him—believing that he'd accidentally dropped it—that Uffa relented and walked away.

Alma changed her mind and became a frequent visitor to the Fox home, eating her meals with the family. She firmly supported Uffa in his ambition to be a designer and builder of racing boats, and at weekends they cruised around the Island together in *Ariel*. On one weekend Uffa casually said to his mother, 'We thought of getting married at Newport Register Office. I thought we could get it over quietly without any fuss because I want to go sailing afterwards. I thought it would be a good idea if we moved in here. There's plenty of room for two in my bedroom.'[85] Arthur Fox was the only witness, and Uffa could find no decent shoes, so he wore a pair of old, battered plimsolls, with one of his toes protruding (one of Uffa's quirks was that he only cut his toenails on Tuesdays). There was no honeymoon or reception, and when the brief ceremony was over, Uffa took the bus to Ryde where he was due to be sailing in a race. When Alma's mother heard the news, later that day,

85   Dixon, June. *UFFA FOX: A Personal Biography*, Angus & Robertson, 1978

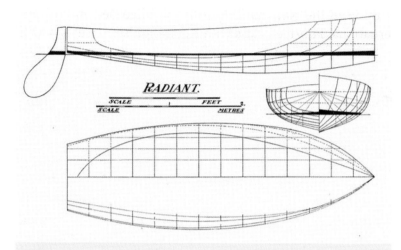

With *Radiant* Uffa arrived at a formula which became the guide for the class for the next thirty years.

she was devastated and became so distressed that her family feared she would throw herself in the river.

As Uffa became more confident, he designed and built *Radiant*, a deeper V-section boat which was fast to windward but unstable, and still didn't really plane. With *Radiant*, however, Uffa evolved a formula which would become standard in the class for the next thirty years: twenty per cent of the sail plan would be in the headsail and the remaining eighty per cent was in the mainsail. Uffa had an equally simple formula for the hull proportions: three beams to a length, which meant that a fifty-six-inch beam would be ideal for a fourteen-foot hull. *Radiant* fell short of his dreams and was not especially easy to sail, but he still managed to come second in the newly created Prince of Wales Cup, which would become, and has remained, the most prestigious of dinghy trophies. The winner was *Irex*, designed and built by Bruce Atkey of Cowes and sailed by his son Cecil, and third was Morgan-Giles in *Vamoosa*.[86]

---

86   https://gbr.international14.org/the-uffa-fox-era-1928-1939/

Radiant

By 1928 the National Fourteen class had become the International Fourteen class with a common set of rules which would remain largely unchanged until the 1970s. As Uffa's reputation grew, so his order book began to fill but, despite the popularity of his designs, he rarely made money from them. Part of the reason was his insistence on the highest standards of materials and workmanship. He was a perfectionist, and his hand-crafted boats were as close to flawless as any boatbuilder of the era could attain. Another reason was that he had expensive tastes and the 'one-third-up-front' deposits he received from customers were often spent long before he had paid his many creditors. Throughout his life Uffa would spend more than he could really afford and rarely settled his bills on time. The townspeople of Cowes always knew if Uffa had banked another cheque. When flush with cash, he had a habit of entering the barber's shop with a shout of, 'I'll pay for everyone if I can go first!' By the time he got back to his yard, there would be a posse of creditors waiting outside his office.

Chapter 6
Avenger

As business increased, Uffa needed both a new home and a new workshop. The Fox family set great store on the value of freehold property, but Uffa's choices were severely limited by his funds. Most men would have looked for two different buildings, but it was typical of Uffa to think that they could be combined. He was an early advocate of the 'work from home' arrangements which became so popular during the Covid lockdowns of 2020 and 2021. He invariably lived above his workshops and rarely wasted time travelling to and from his yard. Throughout his career he would cleverly adapt buildings and premises to his own exacting needs, but his first purchase was novel, even by his standards. He persuaded his father to buy the old Victorian steam-powered Floating Bridge, which had long ago been replaced by a newer model.

Uffa always knew that his family had once owned the exclusive ferry rights over the Medina River, and ever since he was a child, he had loved this remarkable piece of Victorian engineering. 'We boys never wearied of watching and listening to her lovely great steam-engines with their gleaming copper pipes and highly polished steel rods running on the starboard side, while on the port side, the steam came pouring out of the great boilers. Between were two great, cast-iron driving wheels hollowed out to take the links of the chain and fitted with wooden cogs … There were pilots and a great wheel on either side with spokes on it to raise and lower the prows.'[87]

The first Floating Bridge had run from 1859 to 1882 and the second from 1882 to 1909. They were always immaculately maintained and usually very punctual because Queen Victoria and her visitors often used the ferry, as did the soldiers who were based in East Cowes. The third vessel had been built locally by W White & Sons at their Vectis yard. She was the last to be steam-driven, and the last to be run by the privately owned Southampton and Isle of Wight Steam Packet Company. On one occasion, however, she kept the queen waiting and, as a consequence, the rights were transferred to the Isle of Wight County Council by Act of Parliament, 'So that the elder brethren of Cowes could control their own ferry.'[88] During the First World War, the third ferry had been retired and used as spare parts for the fourth Floating Bridge, which had entered service in 1909. It was this third Floating Bridge, now somewhat dilapidated, that Arthur Fox was able to buy in 1925—after some careful negotiating—for just £150 (£7,500 at current values).

At first glance, it seemed a crazy idea and was greeted with laughter by some. But Uffa's conversion of the old vessel was ingenious. He knew she was built of Lomore iron and was not, therefore, as seriously affected by rust as a steel vessel would have been, so her age could be ignored. Her long deck had been designed to take six carriages in line ahead and two abreast, and there were prows at either end that could be raised or lowered, like drawbridges. These could be used by Uffa as ramps, or slipways when it was time to launch a new boat. On either side of the deck had been cabins for the passengers, a wheelhouse for the crew, as well as her steam boiler, engine and coal bunker. This accommodation he cleverly converted into a

87   Fox, Uffa. *Joys of Life*. Newnes. 1966.
88   Ibid.

Floating Bridge & Ferry, Cowes.

drawing office with a twenty-four-foot-wide table, as well as a kitchen, bathroom, dining room and two bedrooms. He collected fresh rainwater from the roof and stored it in the old water tank. The rooms, and especially the drawing office, were spacious and light and the dining room was big enough for Uffa to entertain, which he frequently did. As a boat designer, he knew how to use space efficiently and the bunk beds doubled as chairs and storage. He added a door from the Empress Eugene's yacht to separate his drawing office from his workshop, and the walls were lined with the many books he had collected: 'I have always believed it impossible to feel lonely in a room with books, as we have only to stretch out a hand to find a friend and enrich our lives.'[89] Finally, he had his home towed to Kingston Farm, on the east bank of the Medina, below the Folly. That evening, Alma was seen on the west bank below the gas works, looking perplexed. 'Have you lost something?' asked a workman. 'Yes,' she said, 'my home.'

In his haste to get the old ferry towed to its new mooring, Uffa had neglected to tell her where they now lived. Alma,

---

89   Fox, Uffa. *Joys of Life*. Newnes. 1966.

however, despite many such surprises, would remain a patient and practical wife. She continued to work as a teacher, and in her spare time tried hard to bring order into Uffa's sometimes chaotic business dealings. On occasions, she even had to dip into her teacher's salary to pay Uffa's workmen. In his autobiography, Uffa conceded that Alma had, '... made it all the pleasanter with curtains, flower decorations and the thousand and one little graces that transform a house into a home.'[90]

Before long, the tax collector for the Arreton Parish Council called and demanded payment of the rates. Uffa claimed that Floating Bridge was still a working vessel, temporarily moored, and not therefore a home. The authorities disagreed and issued a summons. Throughout his life, Uffa would fight a series of memorable court cases, usually offering ingenious defences and often winning, but not on this occasion. Nevertheless, Uffa knew that the banks of the Medina River were, at that time, divided between four different local authorities, and it was an easy matter to move the Floating Bridge from one to another. So simple, in fact, that he only had to put his six of his men into *Britannia's* five-oared rowing gig: four to row, one to steer and one to handle lines. With the benefit of the tide and an easterly wind, he slipped his moorings in the Parish of Whippingham and allowed the Floating Bridge to drift west into the parish of Northwood. From there she was towed down the west bank of the Medina until she entered the parish of West Cowes, and finally back across the river to East Cowes, the parish for which Arthur Fox was the official rate collector. This enabled him to write to the council and ask, 'Is it legal for you to collect taxes for the parish of East Cowes and also from the parishes of Northwood and West Cowes, as well as Whippingham, because my Floating Bridge has been in those four parishes during the time in question and is at this moment in East Cowes?' When an astonished

90   Fox, Uffa. *Joys of Life*. Newnes. 1966.

functionary arrived to see for himself, Uffa invited him in for a glass of port, before sending him on his way, empty handed. He heard no more from any of the councils, and a short time later, moved the Floating Bridge back to its original mooring.

Uffa had become less cautious in his designs and finally decided that, with his own drawing office and ample workspace, he would go all the way and try to build a fully planing dinghy. She would be named *Avenger*, after the ill-fated ship on which his grandfather had lost his life, and she would be ready for the 1928 season. *Avenger*, unlike *Ariel* and *Radiant* would have a fully V-sectioned hull. V-sections plane so well that they can actually reduce the boat's displacement by half, which, in turn, can double the speed. The problem with planing hulls, however, is that they only plane well at speed and they are much more affected by heel. U-section boats have rounded hulls, so the wetted area is only slightly increased when heeled, whereas a V shape has significantly more wetted area when at an angle. Uffa knew, from the outset, that he would have to try and avoid excessive heel when sailing to windward, but he would be very fast on a run or reach. He also knew that these advantages would be lost when the windspeed was less than twelve miles an hour: 'She had to be sailed upright at all times excepting in a strong calm when she was listed just enough for the sails to drop naturally into their proper shape, so that the gentle air of a strong calm had not to push the sail at all into its shape, all of its energy being then saved for pushing *Avenger*, and the speeds reached in a strong or a fresh calm were so slow that the shape of the underwater did not matter.'[91]

Uffa later described Avenger's hull in detail, 'Her V sections run down to give her a deep chest forward of midships and run right throughout her length ... The V sections for the first third give her an angle of attack to the water ... so as *Avenger's*

---

91   Fox, Uffa, *Sailing, Seamanship and Yacht Construction,* Peter Davies, 1934.

Avenger

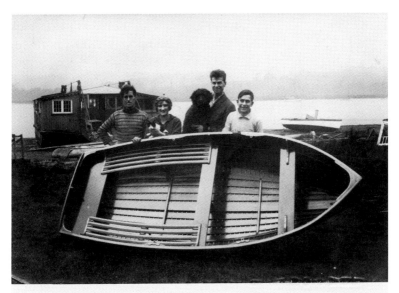

Uffa Fox (far left) with his wife, Alma, presenting an immaculately finished rowing dinghy in front of his Floating Bridge home and workshop.

shaped bow was driven through the water, its shape and angle of attack caused it to lift. The two thirds of length in her long run aft ran fast and easily in the groove cut by the sharp V bow perhaps three inches less in depth than her waterline at rest. She changed trim and went along at double the speed of any other dinghy at this time. It was this planing ability that made her invincible in winds of over twelve miles an hour, and so the first seagoing, planing sailing boat was born.'[92] This was a slight exaggeration, planing dinghies had been built before by other designers, including Morgan-Giles, but none were as fast or as effective as *Avenger*.

Earlier fourteen-footers had gunter lug rig—the older rules prohibited any spar from exceeding the boat's length by more than eighteen inches. At a YRA meeting, Uffa persuaded them to change the rules, allowing him to switch to the more efficient Bermudian rig. However, a fourteen-foot hull was

92   Fox, Uffa, *Sailing Boats*, Newnes, 1959.

Uffa at work in the drawing office of the Floating
Bridge. Image Mike Dixon.

still the largest that could be sent by train, and Uffa's mast was
longer than the maximum that would fit into a goods waggon.
In those days, rail was the most popular way of moving a
dinghy around the country as the railway companies offered
a standard tariff of six shillings to any destination in England.
He overcame the problem by designing a jointed mast that
slotted together like a fishing rod, with the joint being fifteen
feet and six inches from the heel.[93]

A long-standing problem on all boats with drop keels had
been waterproofing the centreboard case. The usual solution
was wooden fillers, but Uffa had come across an old Irish
newspaper, dating from 1898, in which he read that the
class rules for Water Wag dinghies had prohibited the use of
canvas seals. This gave him the idea of persuading the British
Rubber Company to produce tight, overlapping rubber seals,
which eliminated the problem. Another of his innovations
was swivelling extensions on the tillers, enabling helmsmen

93   https://www.classicboat.co.uk/spotlight/uffa-fox-
reflections-on-a-great-sailing-character-by-barry-pickthall

to sit out over the weather side. Like many of Uffa's advances, they are widely used to this day.

From the outset, he put as much weight and gear as possible into the centre of the boat to ensure that bow and stern would easily ride through waves and avoid any tendency to 'dig in'. He put buoyancy tanks in the bilge, amidships, so that any water the boat shipped would not gather in the lee bilge and slow her down. He used cross-tree and double diamond rigging to secure the mast, allowing the jib to be sheeted in, clear of all rigging. Despite all this, it took skill to sail her into the wind: 'The playing of her mainsheet won her many races, for often she would leave other dinghies standing with her mainsail eased off and flying out to leeward like a flag, while they had theirs full of wind, the difference being that they were heeled over and lifeless while *Avenger* was upright and footing fast.'[94]

When the design was at an advanced stage, there was a significant rule change which seriously affected *Avenger*. Designers had previously been allowed to trade off weight for sail, and Uffa planned for Avenger to weigh twenty-seven kilos less than usual with just under a square metre less sail. When the rule was altered, Uffa was forced to add an eighteen-kilo bronze rudder to bring her up to the legal weight.

Despite this setback, her results were staggering. In the 1928 season *Avenger* achieved fifty-two wins, two seconds and three thirds, out of fifty-seven starts.[95] She changed dinghy and yacht sailing forever and was, probably, the most significant racing dinghy ever built.

'Other Fourteens planed on occasions,' wrote Tom Vaughan, the class historian. '*Avenger* would pick up her skirts and go at the slightest provocation—it became the rule rather than the exception. On the wind *Avenger* was just as efficient'. The sport, Uffa's

94   Fox, Uffa, *Sailing, Seamanship and Yacht Construction*, Peter Davies, 1934.
95   Ibid.

competitors joked, was no longer dinghy sailing but Fox hunting.[96]

Uffa was nothing if not impulsive. When he heard from a friend that a major sailing regatta had begun in Le Havre, and it would continue for another three days, he immediately decided to sail *Avenger* across the Channel, persuading Bob Dickerson and Spike Crews to come with him as crew. The next important races in England would be the Prince of Wales and Trent Cups to be held in Lowestoft, and that gave them time to reach Le Havre and return: 'So we thought we would have a dart at the French.'[97]

They loaded the open fourteen-foot boat with three hundredweight of food, clothing and gear, and sailed at four o'clock that very afternoon, making excellent time as far as Bembridge. The journey to France alone would have been a serious challenge for most sailors. While *Avenger* was perfectly at home in the sometimes-challenging waters of the Solent, the English Channel was an entirely different prospect.

Beyond Bembridge the wind came up and the weather worsened. Another sailor might have turned back, but Uffa merely reefed his mainsail and headed straight for Le Havre, close hauled on a starboard tack. Before long they were shipping water faster than two men could bail, but that still did not deter him. He simply eased to leeward sufficiently for one man to be able to bail and continued towards France. At this point they were passed by a much larger cutter, also destined for Le Havre, which had turned back to the Isle of Wight because not even three reefs were enough in these conditions.

By midnight the weather had eased enough for *Avenger* to fully raise her sails. The following day the sun shone but they were soon becalmed and Cap de la Hève did not finally show over the skyline until 6.00 pm.[98] Uffa wrote 'The next morning

96   https://sailcraftblog.wordpress.com/2016/10/05/pt-1-6-fox-hunting-uffa-fox-avenger-and-the-planing-dinghy/
97   Fox, Uffa, *Sailing, Seamanship and Yacht Construction*, Peter Davies, 1934.
98   Ibid.

Avenger flying her prize flags at the end of the 1928 season: fifty-two firsts, two seconds and three thirds out of fifty-seven starts. She was the 'first boat in a new era of sailing'.

we raced and won, as we did again the day after, for the Havre course is in the shadow of la Hève where there are no tricks in the tide. Thursday night I attended the dinner of the Société des Regattes du Havre, feeling rather like our Royal National Lifeboat Institution, for like it, I was supported by voluntary contributions, wearing (not having taken a dinner jacket) Commander Eldred's trousers, a French yachtsman's dinner jacket, another's shoes, but my own handkerchief.'[99]

Uffa was now famous, and his reputation was spreading internationally. His success with *Avenger* would make him the most renowned and influential yacht designer in the world. He would never need to advertise and would almost always have a full order book. Yachtsmen now wrote to him from across the world and they did not need to know his address (which changed whenever he moved the Floating Bridge); they simply had to write: 'Uffa Fox, Cowes, England' on the envelope, and it would always find him.

His ideas would dominate dinghy and small keelboat design for decades and are still influential today. *Avenger* survives and is on permanent display in the Maritime Museum section of Cowes Library, where visitors can see the extraordinary level of fine detail and workmanship that went into her. Uffa's perfectionism made his boats anything from three to five times as expensive as some earlier boats in the class. He rarely made money from them, but his reputation as a boatbuilder was second to none.

The regatta ended on a Thursday but, like many sailors, Uffa was superstitious and would not consider returning to England on Friday the thirteenth. This particular belief was reinforced by his faith: as a choirboy, during long sermons, his imagination would '... wander miles on the wings of thought, and in one of these wanderings I suddenly came face to face with the fact, that people fear Fridays because of the first Good Friday, and thirteen because that was the number

---

99   Fox, Uffa, *Sailing, Seamanship and Yacht Construction,* Peter Davies, 1934.

Avenger

Avenger is preserved at the Cowes Heritage Museum in the public library, Beckford Road, Cowes.

at the Last Supper'.[100] Throughout his life he would refuse to dine with thirteen at the table, and one of his secretaries recalls being sent out at the last minute to find a fourteenth guest at Uffa's insistence. Among the sailing community in Cowes, he was not alone. The legendary boatbuilder, Clare Lallow, would never agree to launch any boat on a Friday, no matter how urgently it was needed.

They set sail for Cowes on the Saturday morning. Once again, they found themselves in challenging conditions. The wind was from the north-east, dead ahead. It was gentle at first but soon hardened although the sea remained relatively flat. Four hours later, however, they had to reef sails as they were shipping so much water. With all three men completely outside the boat, except for their legs below the knees, the strain on the rigging was such that Uffa feared the shrouds would break and dismast them. He would later recall, '... but

100   Fox, Uffa, *Sailing, Seamanship and Yacht Construction*, Peter Davies, 1934.

83

as a faint heart never won a fat woman we let *Avenger* stand it, until the sea made up enough to force us into reefing. Just before dark we lifted the Island on our weather bow, and continuing on our port tack, later saw the Owers flashing out dead ahead.' [101]

The Owers Lightvessel was anchored seven miles southeast of Selsey Bill, and ten miles west of Bembridge.[102] As they went about, close to the Lightvessel, they took a wave so big that they were almost swamped. Both their hurricane lamp and electric lamp went out and everything in the boat, including their matches, was soaked. They were now in a busy shipping lane in bad weather, at night, without any lights. There were shoals inside the Owers, which Uffa thought he could navigate, but soon realised it was hopeless in these conditions. He tacked close inshore, just above Bembridge, and in the first light of dawn they saw the old church of St Helens. They beat on to Seaview Pier where they made fast and went ashore.

Uffa thought nothing of knocking on the door of the first cottage they came to, having seen smoke rising from the chimney, and asking if they could have breakfast. He recalled, 'While this was being cooked, we all three fell asleep on the lawn, which was wet with dew, but as we were wet through, we did not mind this. Bob and Spike had been bailing all night, and I had been steering for seventeen hours, so we were extremely tired, and even *Avenger* had felt the strain, for she had altered shape forward, and ever after was faster in wind and sea. After breakfast we sailed to Ryde, but our race was not until the afternoon, by which time the wind had died, leaving but the faintest of airs, in which our tired brains refused to sparkle, so we finished third to Tom Thornycroft and A C Walker. Then away for Cowes where

101   Fox, Uffa, *Sailing, Seamanship and Yacht Construction*, Peter Davies, 1934.
102   There are no longer any manned lightships on the British coast; all have been replaced by automatic beacons.

the Customs allowed us to keep the three small bottles of scent, as we had opened them, and explained that they were for our own adornment. *Avenger* had taken twenty-nine hours to sail to Havre, and thirty-seven hours to beat back. Bob and Spike have bronze medals, whilst I have a silver one and a cup to remind us of *Avenger*'s greatness, all of which she won at Havre.'[103]

Back in Cowes, Uffa consolidated his team of craftsmen. His Chief Draughtsman and old Sea Scout friend, Bill Waight, had married Alma's sister, Vera, making the two men brothers-in-law. Throughout his life Uffa would favour employing family members, close friends, or those who displayed the character traits he most admired—especially loyalty and adaptability. In his autobiography, written towards the end of his life, he would say that this was the beginning of his happiest years.

Not only did he look for the finest artisans, but he wanted them all to be good sailors too. If you worked for Uffa, you never knew when you might be expected to crew for him, or for a customer. He was a very demanding employer, but he often inspired great devotion in his men. In his autobiography, he recorded how he came to hire Arthur Keeping, better known as Buster, who worked for him for twenty-five years and remained a friend for life. Uffa had telephoned Fearon and Sons to order an oil lamp and Buster had been dispatched to the Floating Bridge, a two-mile walk in each direction, to deliver it. Uffa held it to the light and saw two tiny holes. He recalled, 'I kicked Arthur Keeping in the arse, asked him to look up through to see if he could see these pinpricks of light, and he replied that he could.'

Buster was sent back to the shop and ordered to return with another, which he did, having now walked six miles. This time he held it to the light himself to confirm that there were no holes. Uffa thanked him for the second lamp before giving

103   Fox, Uffa, *Sailing, Seamanship and Yacht Construction*, Peter Davies, 1934.

85

the boy sixpence and sending him on his way. Buster replied, 'May I come and work for you, mister?' When Uffa asked him why, he said, 'Well, I shall always know where I am with you. I shall either get a kick in the arse or sixpence. I have never seen anyone as definite as you before, and my father says I need directing on my way through life by an exacting person.' Uffa immediately offered him a job with the sole proviso that Fearon and Sons were happy to release him, which they were.

The boy lived in Arctic Road in West Cowes, on the opposite bank of the Medina, which meant he had a two-mile walk and a ferry trip in each direction. He and his brother built a pram dinghy and Buster rowed it back and forth, every day, in fair weather and foul. Uffa recalled, 'It was a wonderful sight to see him rowing up the river in this little, short pram in a southerly gale with the wind against tide, for then she often stood up on end like a sentry box in the waves.'

Buster completed a seven-year apprenticeship and a few years later told Uffa that he was getting married. One of Uffa's firm beliefs was that every married man should own the freehold of his home. He told Buster to go with his fiancée and find a house, and when he had done so a way would be found to help him pay for it. Uffa often lent his men the deposit for a home and allowed them to repay it over many years. Decades later, after World War II, Buster wanted to sell the house, which had now quadrupled in value, but felt he needed Uffa's permission. Uffa gave his consent but, in the end. Buster decided to stay where he and his wife had always been happy.

Alma continued to work as a relief teacher, helping out at schools across the Isle of Wight. She travelled everywhere by bus, changing her boots for shoes at the bus stop. When at home on the Floating Bridge, she was a popular intermediary between Uffa and his men. Alma knew how to pour oil onto troubled water, especially during Uffa's periodic bad moods, which could last for days at a time. At the same time, she looked after his paperwork and administration, something Uffa cared little for. Throughout his career he would always delegate office work to secretaries and assistants. He dictated his rambling and highly personal letters into a machine and typists transcribed them for him—later he would do the same for the books he wrote. He rarely took a personal interest in any deskwork that didn't involve designing boats.

Avenger was followed by *Daring*, in which Uffa tried to further increase the planing ability of a fourteen-footer. Although he won the Prince of Wales Cup, the Trent Island Waterways Challenge Cup, and the Lowestoft Fifty Guinea Cup in *Daring*, Uffa felt that he had sacrificed too much weatherliness for the additional speed, and he began to consider producing larger keelboats in future. Just how difficult *Daring* was to sail in some conditions, is vividly illustrated in Uffa's first book, *Sailing, Seamanship and Yacht Construction*: 'The last round, [of the Prince of Wales Cup] however, was almost fatal to us; as we were about to gybe round the Duke Rock Buoy my crew stood up, and being unable to see and afraid of hitting the buoy, I let *Daring* luff. Bringing that weight of wind abeam, with no one on the gunwale, caused *Daring* to scoop herself (at that speed) practically full of water. So full she would have sunk with two aboard, but my crew jumped overboard and floating outside bailed from there, while I bailed from inside, steering all the while. We drifted to leeward of the Duke Rock without rounding it, and tried to tack in order to weather it, just as soon as the water was low enough to allow my crew back aboard, but *Daring* would not have it. There was no time to waste for Tom in *Pintail* was roaring up all the while, so we had to gybe *Daring* which was like a log in the water. Once at the Duke Rock we gybed her again, still sluggish and dangerously full of water, and once round heaved a sigh of relief, and reached for the Asia buoy and the finishing line, winning by less than one-and-a-half minutes.'[104]

---

104   Fox, Uffa, *Sailing, Seamanship and Yacht Construction*, Peter Davies, 1934.

Uffa Fox's Daring K201. The International Fourteen in
which he won the 1929 Prince of Wales Cup.

The old Floating Bridge had evolved into an unusual but
comfortable home. It was surrounded by open countryside
and Uffa could ramble and hunt at leisure, often shooting
rabbits and game birds for the pot. He had always loved dogs

and, by now, had three, who accompanied him everywhere. There were always boats moored close by that he could sail or row as he chose. His favourite was *Rocket*, an Edwardian steam launch. Her copper tube boiler could produce twenty-five pounds of pressure in fifteen minutes, and to Uffa's eye, the cat's cradle of her pipes was as beautiful as the tracery of a cathedral window. Uffa had loved steam power since first seeing the Floating Bridge as a boy, and he regretted its passing. In spring and summer, he would steam in *Rocket* to Newtown Creek and enjoy the undisturbed bird and wildlife. In winter he used her for fishing and duck shooting.

At that time, dinghies were moved around the country primarily by rail—a fourteen-footer fitted comfortably into a goods waggon—and Uffa's customers lived the length and breadth of the United Kingdom. Incredibly, the boats were never packed into crates, or even protected in any way; they travelled exactly as they were. Uffa had a soft spot for railwaymen and trusted them to treat his boats gently. In almost every case, they did, and he rarely had any problems with damage in transit. In fact, the Southern Railway sometimes displayed his beautiful craft on the concourse at Waterloo Station so that the travelling public could admire them!

Uffa would always have expensive tastes which were usually beyond his means. He had long ago fallen in love with an old schooner, the *Black Rose*, which he had crewed on many times as a Sea Scout. She had been built in Stornoway in 1860 and originally traded between the Western Isles of Scotland. Her hull shape and rig were unchanged, and she sported a cutwater bow, carved figurehead, and bowsprit. Uffa now purchased her and modified her to his liking, but she was a costly luxury. Her hull needed to be cleaned, repaired and repainted, but rather than going to the expense of hiring a dry dock, or crane, he used the ancient method of careening. He and his men took *Black Rose*, broadside on, close to the bank and, as the tide ebbed and the river level dropped, she grounded. This meant they could list her first to port, and then—on the next tide—to starboard, each time exposing enough of her hull for the work to be completed. For safety, however, they needed calm conditions—if she was disturbed by wash just as she was being lifted from the ground, she could be wrecked.

At a critical moment, a fast Royal Navy vessel began to conduct high-speed tests along the Medina's measured mile. On the bridge of the warship were shipyard managers and Royal Naval overseers, but they ignored (or simply didn't hear) the shouts that came from the men working on *Black Rose*. Uffa had a volcanic temper at the best of times but, on this occasion, his rage knew no bounds. An apprentice was ordered to run back to the Floating Bridge and fetch—of all things—a four-bore rifle. Uffa must have been one of the few men in the country to still own and use such a weapon. The four-bore was a Victorian black powder gun which fired a massive one-inch diameter bullet and was used to hunt very large animals, including elephants! The cartridges were so powerful that during the Second World War they were used to start the biggest aircraft engines. When Uffa began to fire rounds across the navy ship's bows, her crew got the hint and sailed away to the safety of Osborne Bay.

Uffa's eccentricities were well known on the Isle of Wight and, on the whole, tolerated; he was, after all, a local hero. On this occasion, however, voices were demanding he be prosecuted. It was time, the shipyard managers felt, that Uffa Fox was shown that he didn't actually own the river. The debate rumbled on, but Uffa had many influential friends, including the Harbour Master and the Chief Constable. In the event, nothing happened, and the 'Elephant Gun' incident became another part of Uffa's considerable legend.

By 1930, Uffa was the undisputed grandmaster of dinghy design. In that year's Prince of Wales Cup, six of his fourteen-

Avenger

My Old Schooner " Black Rose."

WITH BEST WISHES
from UFFA FOX,
COWES, ENGLAND.

91

footers won five first places while competing against more than fifty entrants. On returning to Cowes from Lowestoft, Uffa was jubilant, but his father quickly put him in his place. 'There were six of your boats in the race but only five were in the first six … you should have seen to it that your six boats took the first six places.'[105]

Uffa felt the need for a new challenge, and he decided to try his hand at designing and building a larger keelboat for entry into a Swedish regatta, which would be based on the Skerry Cruiser rules. Built under the relatively relaxed 'Square Metre Rule', Skerry Boats had originated in Sweden and were popular in the Baltic. The liberal class rules gave designers considerable freedom and allowed them to push the sailboat technology of the era to its limits. The 'Square Metre Rule' meant that yachts were classed primarily by their sail area, which was fixed. There were few other limitations, but there were minimum requirements for weight and cabin measurements. *Vigilant*, a fixed-keel Bermudian rigged racing yacht, was thirty-four feet and six inches overall, twenty-five feet and six inches at the waterline, and she displaced two tonnes. She was roughly the same size as a six-metre yacht, but with half the displacement and half the sail area, making her very fast but not ideally suited to deep water sailing. That having been said, no sooner was her varnish dry than Uffa thought nothing of sailing her to Sweden, along with his old Sea Scout friend, Bob Dickerson, and Dr R T Cooke, owner of the yacht *Enid*. Cooke's yacht would later be wrecked—with all crew saved—during the 1933 Round the Island Race, which Uffa won as helmsman of *Daedalus,* a sixty-year-old cutter.

They encountered five storms during the round trip to Sweden, and Uffa noted, with satisfaction, 'While chasing away before three of these gales, she seemed to tear along at twice her natural speed, which suggests that her press of sail was three times as much as she should carry. *Vigilant* did not

---

105   Fox, Uffa, *Joys of Life*, Newnes, 1966.

suffer at all through this harsh treatment, except that the paint came off her seams under water near her entrance, which would have happened to any new vessel, and is the reason for not coppering a new ship until she is a year or so old, and settled down in life.'[106]

The Swedish regatta was a very grand affair, describing itself as the 'European Meeting of all Nations' and designed to celebrate the Swedish Yacht Club's centenary. More than 500 yachts had been entered, some owned and sailed by royalty, including Prince Olaf of Norway. Uffa's voyage across the North Sea in a light yacht that was clearly not ideal for the journey drew a lot of attention, and the Royal Swedish Yacht Club presented him with a special trophy for an 'outstanding cruise'. This was as well, because he won nothing else.

Uffa recorded the voyage in his book, *Sailing, Seamanship and Yacht Construction*. They left in fine weather and the book includes a photograph of Uffa, standing naked in the prow, while taking a sextant reading. He captioned the image, 'Modesty is only a sense of physical imperfection.' However, as they passed the German coast, a heavy squall blew up. With two reefs in her mainsail *Vigilant* was still able make six knots into the wind. The following morning, they were becalmed but, when the gentlest of breezes came up, *Vigilant* was able to make one knot. The calm was followed by thick fog, although, once the sun had burned it away, a good breeze took them into the Kiel Canal, along which they were able to make eight knots. After stopping for two days in Kiel, they continued across the Baltic in fierce storms, finally arriving in Sandhamn—a small harbour close to Stockholm—in time for the last four days of the eighteen-day regatta.

In the first race they finished a lowly eighth, which Uffa put down to being more used to nimble fourteen-footers. 'It was not until the last race that I realised that we lost so much

---

106   Fox, Uffa, *Sailing, Seamanship and Yacht Construction*, Peter Davies, 1934.

(Opposite) Vigilant under construction on the Floating Bridge.

(Left Clockwise) Uffa Fox, Bob Dickerson, and Dr R T Cooke prepare to leave Cowes.

(Below) Competing in Sweden.

Vigilant was restored in 2010 and she returned to Cowes for the UF50 celebration in 2022.

each time we tacked, and I had been tacking far too much, and never in my life have I made a good start. We were up against the finest of helmsmen, and what more could a man desire?'[107] It was a disappointing regatta. *Vigilant* did not reach the podium in any of the races. She was a beautiful and fast boat—remarkably seaworthy for her size and weight—but she was no match for the competition. Nonetheless, everyone admired Uffa for his seamanship in having reached Sweden in the first place. British Pathé even produced a special newsreel to mark the event, showing a smiling Uffa on the deck of *Vigilant* wearing wing collar, tie and white duck trousers, but he could not repeat the glory he had earned in smaller boats. Uffa recalled feeling sad as he sailed past the Royal Swedish Yacht Club for the last time and dipped his ensign in farewell.

Vigilant returned to Cowes in 2022 for the UF50 anniversary, and *Yachts and Yachting* magazine wrote, 'At a time when offshore yachts were slab-sided, heavy, often overbuilt and with prodigious internal volume, taking on a blue water gale in a slender, needle-nosed, ultra-light boat with around three metres of overhang forward and aft and barely any freeboard like *Vigilant* would be generally regarded as foolhardy ... at best. For Fox, though, the way *Vigilant* handled the rolling mountains of green water and hammer-blasts of the North Sea storm confirmed his personal design view and ultimately influenced the evolution of offshore yacht design. "[She] is just what you need for the rough waters found along the British coast. The volume in the ends of the boat makes it rise lightly and elegantly like a sea swallow over the waves," he wrote afterwards.'[108]

In 1931, Uffa was offered the chance to crew in a race across the Atlantic from west to east. 'Paul Hammond's invitation to form one of *Landfall*'s crew for the Transatlantic

---

107   Fox, Uffa, *Sailing, Seamanship and Yacht Construction,* Peter Davies, 1934.
108   Dewar, Oliver, *Game changing Uffa Fox design* Vigilant *is for sale at the UF50 festival, Yachts and Yachting*, 13 Aug 2022.

Race was accepted like a shot as, besides the honour the invitation carried, there was in store the joy of crewing on a vessel whose owner aimed at perfection in every detail from lead keel to truck.'[109] The race would be from the Brenton Reef lightship (at the entrance to Narragansett Bay, Rhode Island) to Plymouth Breakwater, a distance of three-thousand nautical miles.

At seventy feet overall, the ketch *Landfall* was considerably larger and more comfortable than either *Typhoon* or *Diablesse*. In fact, her cabin fittings came close to luxury. There were two bathrooms along with bookshelves, gun cases, and even a small piano. Uffa enthused about her design but disliked her transom stern: 'While the faults of a transom stern are not noticeable in smooth water they are in a seaway, where it drags dead water behind it level with the rail each time the bow rises on a sea. The words:

> "——*that the currents of parted seas,*
> *Closing behind with mighty force,*
> *Might aid and not impede her course.*"[110]

express every designer's aim, as the way a vessel leaves the water is of greater importance than the way in which she cleaves it.'[111]

On this trip, Uffa was the sail trimmer, not the navigator, but that didn't prevent him giving an opinion on the best route. He favoured the Great Circle track, just skirting Nova Scotia, because it was two hundred miles shorter, and he believed it had stronger and more reliable winds; *Typhoon* had crossed by this route in just fifteen days. However, an article had recently appeared in the American magazine *Yachting* which favoured the southern and Gulf Stream course. Uffa

---

109   Fox, Uffa, *Sailing, Seamanship and Yacht Construction*, Peter Davies, 1934.
110   Longfellow, Henry Wadsworth, *The Seaside and the Fireside*, 1850.
111   Fox, Uffa, *Sailing, Seamanship and Yacht Construction*, Peter Davies, 1934.

lobbied as hard as he knew for the northern route, even showing people copies of Bill Nutting's book, *The Track of the Typhoon*, but to little avail. '... the Gulf Stream, with its promise of a free ride, was strong magic, so everyone seemed after the southern course.'[112] Paul Hammond insisted on it and Uffa, for once, had to acquiesce. For all the arguing, Uffa noted in his diary, '*Landfall* a very happy ship, everyone keen to win, and all thoughtful for the rest on board.'[113]

They made a good fast crossing but arrived in Plymouth to find that Olin Stephens' *Dorade* had berthed two days before them. Stephens had taken the northern route, which, Uffa felt, vindicated his choice. *Dorade* had been greatly helped by a generous handicap but, in the end, had not needed it. *Landfall* was third, with all ten entrants in the race arriving safely and no lives lost. *Dorade* was a lightly built fifty-two-foot ketch; so fragile, in fact, that the banker and philanthropist George Roosevelt (a distant relative of President Theodore 'Teddy' Roosevelt) had questioned whether she should have been allowed to enter such a challenging race at all. Uffa was much impressed by her and, as always, learned lessons from her design: 'Off the wind *Dorade* is as fast as a ten-metre, and to windward half a minute a mile slower, and reaching across the Sound this summer in a smart breeze the twelve-metres had difficulty in dropping us astern. So *Dorade* is fast beyond all doubt, all possible doubt whatever.'[114]

On the home front, Alma had been struggling, partly because Uffa was never happier than when sailing offshore: 'There is nothing I know of on this earth that can stir a man's imagination and make him feel so humble as being far out at sea in a small sailing vessel, because the sea has remained unchanged from the beginning of time. The sea is great and powerful, and the strength of those on board and that of

---

112   Fox, Uffa, *Sailing, Seamanship and Yacht Construction*, Peter Davies, 1934.
113   Ibid.
114   Ibid.

their ship is small in comparison, so, once afloat, all of us are overawed by the beauty, majesty and power of the sea itself.'

Uffa would later boast, 'From its earliest days this [boatyard] was arranged to run in my absence after I'd completed designs, ordered and seen delivered all timbers, materials and fittings required to complete the vessels, and that their construction was well under way. When I was away the chief draughtsman took over command, if he was away the foreman-boatbuilder, then the foreman fitter, until finally, if he was the only one at work, the youngest apprentice was in control. This enabled me to sail three times across the broad Atlantic and sail the Baltic and visit most of Europe.'[115] In reality, Alma, who was still working as a teacher, had to deal with many problems and, at times, had to use her meagre salary to pay Uffa's men. Alma's family refused to lend her money but, when things were really desperate, they sent her food parcels.

Despite a full order book, Uffa was losing money. His exquisitely built boats cost more to make than he charged his customers, and as orders grew the problems actually worsened—there are few economies of scale when hand-building complicated boats from wood. Added to this, Uffa liked to spend money freely, especially as he now rubbed shoulders with moneyed friends.

Towards the end of his life, Uffa began to write his autobiography. Always an optimist and a positive thinker, he had no regrets and began the book with, 'There are some people who say sadly, "I would like to live my life all over again, knowing what I know now." I am not one of those. I have had such a wonderful life that I should like to live every minute of it all over again. I should like to make all the same mistakes and endure all the same heartaches, because just as we have to be hungry to enjoy a good meal so we most know sorrow to enjoy happiness. A good picture must have light and shade, and so surely a full life must have many contrasts … I have been as happy as any king could be …'[116]

---

115   Fox, Uffa, *Joys of Life*, Newnes, 1966.
116   Ibid.

Dorade was a fifty-two-foot ketch so fragile that some questioned whether she should have been allowed to sail the Atlantic at all.

Chapter 7
Sailing Canoes

Uffa had made a wise decision when he chose to build boats for the popular and growing Fourteen-Foot Class. It had made his reputation internationally, and the races were now dominated by his designs. For example, in the Prince of Wales Cup—the most prestigious of all dinghy trophies—it was not unusual for all of the first five or six boats to have been built by him. Nevertheless, in spite of his success, he had never forgotten (and still sailed) the first boat he had ever built: a sixteen-foot sailing canoe constructed from one of S E Saunders' hydroplanes. Sailing canoes were very fast, could be handled by a single crew member, and could be transported on the roof of a car and launched from practically anywhere. Sometimes called the 'Dry Fly' of sailing, in terms of affordability and adaptability, they beat dinghies hands down. In Uffa's opinion, no other boat called for the level of skill needed to sail one effectively, and he campaigned, unsuccessfully, for sailing canoes to become an Olympic class.

In Britain, there had been a craze for sailing canoes in the nineteenth century, inspired by John McGregor's 1865 book, *A Thousand Miles in the Rob Roy Canoe*. By the 1930s, however, the enthusiasm had petered out and the success of fourteen-foot dinghies (thanks in no small part to Uffa Fox) had hastened their demise. But in North America, sailing

Sailing Canoes

canoes remained very popular and Uffa yearned to try out his ideas there. He designed and built two sailing canoes: *East Anglian* for himself, and *Valiant* for his friend, Roger de Quincy (still a student at Oxford), with the aim of challenging for the American Canoe Championship and the New York Canoe Club International Trophy. The latter prize had been won by an American every year since its inception in 1866. This was in spite of several challenges from eminent British canoeists, including the Sea Scouts founder, Warrington Baden-Powell, who had pioneered sailing canoe designs, developing them from the 'Rob Roy' touring concept into racers. Having won the two most important British trophies, the two men left for Canada aboard the *Empress of Britain*. As usual, Uffa was seasick for the first few days—even on a luxurious passenger liner of 42,000 tonnes—an indication of how badly he suffered from the malady![117]

Like his successful dinghies, Uffa's canoe designs were full-blown racing boats with deep-chested V-section planing hulls. They had no keels; the helmsman used a sliding seat to place his weight far enough to windward to counteract heel. The American and British rules were different at the time, so Uffa was hampered by the need to build boats that met both regimes, but was confident that the advantage of planing would be so great that they could still win.

They began in Canada, where they took three first and three second places in six championship races. In the United States they won both of the National Canoe Championships: the sailing championship, and the combined paddling and sailing championship. Finally, in Long Island Sound, they won the New York Canoe Club's International Trophy, the first non-Americans to do so in the race's history. Before they left, they persuaded the Americans to consider changes that would lead to standardised international rules, making the sport a

117   The *Empress of Britain* later became the largest ship to be lost in World War II when she was torpedoed by a German U-Boat on 28 October 1940.

UFFA FOX WINNING THE FINAL RACE FOR THE INTERNATIONAL CANOE TROPHY, 1933

fully international one for the first time. Their tour had been a triumph, and British canoeists would retain the International Trophy for twenty years, but despite the rule changes, canoe sailing would remain a minor sport in Britain, although it would enjoy renewed interest during the final decades of the twentieth century.

Sailing Canoes

Apart from the trophies, however, Uffa would receive little reward for the work he did in canoes, and he sold few of them. It is a mark of his passion for sailing that he worked hardest in the classes that he really believed in, rather than those he knew would pay well. Uffa would have lifelong financial problems, partly through the uncompromising quality of his boats, partly because he never ran his yard for purely financial motives and partly because he spent too freely. But he always put his reputation first, and his reputation has grown in the years since he retired.

Among Uffa's many skills was a gift for words which, at its best, came close to poetry. Throughout his life he wrote magazine and newspaper articles, not only about sailing, but also the countryside, field sports and, occasionally, politics and current affairs. It was only a matter of time before a canny publisher would spot an opportunity for a book.

Peter Lewellyn Davies could hardly have come from a more literary background. A cousin of Daphne du Maurier, he and his brothers were befriended by J M Barrie when, as infants, their nurse walked them in Kensington Gardens. Peter would be the inspiration for Barrie's *Peter Pan*, the legendary and timeless children's story that made a fortune for its author. By the age of thirteen both of Davies' parents had died of cancer and Barrie formally adopted him, becoming his foster father, and sending him to Eton College. Davies won an MC fighting in the trenches of the First World War but, like so many others, suffered emotional damage which scarred him for life, especially when his older brother, George, was killed. Before the war ended, he had fallen in love with the painter and illustrator, Vera Willoughby, wife of the actor Louis Willoughby. Vera was Davies' senior by twenty-seven years and had a daughter older than him, but they openly lived together and, although the relationship scandalised his family—including Barrie—Davies stayed with her for several years.[118]

In spite of the affair, Barrie lent his adopted son the money to start his own publishing house, Peter Davies Ltd, but he bequeathed most of his fortune to the Great Ormond Street Hospital. Throughout his life, Davies would resent his association with *Peter Pan*, describing it as 'that terrible masterpiece'. He had expected to inherit the bulk of Barrie's estate, viewing it as compensation for the public scrutiny he had endured as 'The Boy Who Would Not Grow Up', and would always begrudge the fact that he was only left an annuity. Although Davies created a successful publishing house, he remained an unhappy man and an alcoholic. In 1960, after drinking at the bar of the Royal Court Hotel, he walked to the nearby Sloane Square Underground Station, and threw himself under a train. He was sixty-three years old.

In the early 1930s, however, Peter Davies, like all good publishers, was on the lookout for fresh talent. A new, growing publishing house cannot rely solely on the manuscripts directly offered by authors or their agents—Davies had an eye for good writing and knew how to encourage those who might create it. In 1931, having got over his love affair with Vera Willoughby, he married the socialite daughter of Lord Ruthven, Margaret Leslie Hore-Ruthven. Margaret, and her twin sister, Alison, had shocked London society by founding what newspapers dubbed 'The Bright Young Things', a group of fashionable young socialites whose dress and behaviour scandalised older generations. Both girls were celebrated for their looks and had been featured in Cecil Beaton's *The*

---

118   Vera Willoughby (also known as Vera Petrovna) claimed to have been born and educated in Budapest. In truth, she hailed from South Norwood and trained at The Slade. She fabricated the Hungarian persona to make herself seem more colourful and avant-garde. Her paintings were often erotic and shocked many at the time. Original works by Willoughby are in the collections of the Victoria and Albert Museum and the London Transport Museum.

Book of Beauty. Beaton described them as: 'Byzantine goddesses, dressed like fairies in a circus design by Picasso, with their dark locks tied with little tinsel bows, their spangled ballet-skirts, and low-heeled shoes.' At a coming-of-age party for Loel Guinness, the twins had outraged mondain London by wearing extremely short, tight-fitting dresses in silver lamé. When they started dancing on stage under the name, the Ralli Twins, their parents finally reigned them in (profes-

Peter Davies was the publisher who persuaded Uffa to begin a second career as an author.

sional dancers were then considered little better than prostitutes) and steered them towards suitable husbands. Margaret was a sparkling, beautiful and intelligent woman whose risqué reputation had drawn Peter like a moth to a candle.

The Ruthven family owned a home in Bembridge and Peter regularly holidayed there with his wife. While on the Island, he met Uffa socially and the men quickly became firm friends. Despite coming from opposite ends of society, each recognised the other as an iconoclast, *enfant terrible* and original thinker who delighted in shocking prigs. For the rest of his life, Uffa would consider Peter Davies one of his closest friends and he was proud to be godfather to Peter's second son, George.

Peter immediately saw that that Uffa could write a great book and was famous enough for it to sell, but, initially, could not persuade him to do so. Uffa enjoyed writing (or dictating) short articles but was not certain that he had the staying power to finish a full-length work. Peter gently coaxed and persisted, but Uffa would not be convinced until he received a personal visit from the manager of the Midland Bank. A trip to the Floating Bridge was necessary because Uffa visited the bank himself as rarely as he could. Rodney Barton remembers often being sent to the bank on a Friday to collect the wages. The bank staff would go into a huddle in the corner and there would be a long, whispered debate before the envelope was finally handed to him.

The manager knew that Uffa was about to depart on one his voyages to America, and also knew he had a habit of emptying the coffers before he travelled, leaving the hapless Alma to deal with the consequences. Uffa had received many such visits and usually plied his creditors with vintage port and flattery until the luckless guest staggered away empty handed. On this occasion, however, hospitality was firmly refused and a simple message delivered: unless he immediately reduced his overdraft, the bank would foreclose and Uffa's business would be wound up. It was clear that the manager could no longer be charmed or dissuaded and, when he left, Uffa was in complete despair. Reluctantly, he dispatched a telegram to Peter Davies at his London office: 'Send contract and advance pay by return and I'll sign up.' Uffa Fox was about to become an author.

Uffa could write exquisitely and spontaneously about the things that moved him. He always had notepads and pencils close to hand and had kept a diary all his life, recording all of his sea journeys and describing the rigs and characteristics of the many boats he had sailed in and seen. He began by writing to naval architects across the world for permission to use drawings of their yachts. They all agreed, even his old nemesis, Morgan-Giles, and his first book was lavishly illustrated with their designs along with pictures from the storied photographers, Beken of Cowes, who had (and still have) an unrivalled library of sailing photographs dating back to the nineteenth century.

The resulting book, *Sailing, Seamanship and Yacht Construction*, was rapturously received by critics and public alike, and is still considered a classic. No one wrote about Uffa better than he wrote about himself, and the best appraisal of the book comes from his own pen: 'Sailing, and so Seamanship, will endure until the end of all things, for sailing is the one thing above all others that offers peace and escape to a man whose brain is weary and tired of the machinery which this age and future ages force and will force upon human beings. A few years ago there was peace and pleasure upon the roads of England; to-day the advent and perfection of the motor car, besides destroying this peace and quietude, destroys

those on the road. But the sea has remained, and will remain to the end, much as it was in the beginning, and I believe the spirit still moves upon the waters, and always will …'

Uffa would continue to write for the rest of his life and the books would provide an important and, sometimes, essential supplement to his income. It is an irony that we probably have the Midland Bank to thank for some of the finest writing on sailing and the sea that we know.

His literary reputation opened another career path as a lecturer and public speaker, especially to university students. He was a compelling narrator, and his ribald yarns went down well with most—but not all—audiences. Uffa always enjoyed practical jokes and one lecture he gave to Cambridge students was followed by a drinking session and the kind of high jinks that Oxbridge undergraduates are famous for. He was spotted by the police swinging from a wall bracket while trying to put out a streetlight. The younger men fled but Uffa was caught and taken to a police station where he unsuccessfully tried to convince them he was a visiting poet. A summons was issued and Uffa's response would become one of the many remarkable legal encounters that helped to forge his legend:

> Dear Sir,
> Thank you very much indeed for the summons to appear before your court. I am sorry that as I have another arrangement on that day regretfully I am unable to attend. Will you please thank the policeman who arrested me for being so kind. He did his duty well, being firm as well as kind.
> A friend tells me that the charge for putting out lights is five shillings, so I am enclosing a cheque for thirty shillings and would like you to place the balance in the Police Orphanage Fund.
> With best wishes,
> Yours sincerely, Uffa Fox

The magistrate imposed a fine of £2, in response to which Uffa wrote:

> Dear Sir,
> Thank you very much indeed for the fine, and I enclose a further cheque for £1, which regretfully now only leaves you with a balance of ten shillings to be devoted to the Police Orphanage Fund.
> Best wishes,
> Yours sincerely, Uffa Fox

Sailing Canoes

The story got into the newspapers, much to Uffa's embarrassment and annoyance. Pathé News received a firm no when they asked if they could film Uffa aboard the Floating Bridge.

In the late 1930s, Looe Sailing Club commissioned Uffa to design a sailing dinghy that would be cheap, but seaworthy enough for the challenging seas off South Cornwall. 'Having enjoyed and endured the tumbling seas on the Cornish coast I was in full agreement with the Commodore when he outlined the type of fourteen-footer he would like … and delighted at the prospect of designing such a boat.'

Uffa came up with a fourteen-foot-long (4.27m) boat of clinker construction, well-stayed rig and with a heavy iron centreplate to provide stability. Uffa's Redwing had the ability to keep a sea and also plane off the wind. After the war the Redwing's popularity grew and in 1947 it became the principal local One-Design racing class, known as the 'West of England Conference Redwing'.[119] In 1954 the RYA adopted the Redwing as a 'National' class. In 1988 there was a resurgence of new Redwings being built both in Cornwall and also North America. Redwing Number 1—now approaching eighty years old—is still regularly racing near her birthplace in Cornwall.[120]

Uffa's reputation was (and still is) based principally on his dinghies and small keel boats, but he liked to design and build larger yachts when the opportunity arose. Alan Colman was heir to the Colman's Mustard fortune and Uffa was delighted when Colman commissioned an eighty-three-foot, sixty-ton, ketch from him. The two men began by sketching a full-size plan on the lawn of Colman's Norfolk home. Back in Cowes, Uffa worked with his chief draughtsman and brother-in-law, Bill Waight, to turn the idea into working drawings. Uffa had never qualified as a naval architect, but Bill Waight had, and it was Bill who would produce most of Uffa's drawings.

119   Uffa's 'Looe Redwing' should not be confused with Charles Nicholson's earlier 'Bembridge Redwing'.
120   https://nationalredwing.com/forum/

Colman wanted the yacht to have a steel hull, a material that Uffa had not previously worked in. He went to his old night school mentor, Arthur Brading, Chief Draughtsman of the White Shipyard, for advice. Welded-steel hulls, which had not previously been used on a yacht of that size, were then considered to be state-of-the-art technology, and Whites were keen to manufacture the hull on Uffa's behalf. The new vessel was to be named *Wishbone*, after the style of gaff rig she would use to fly her nearly 3,000 square feet of sail.[121] Uffa had been fascinated by wishbone rig ever since he had seen the ketch *Vamarie* sail past him in Oyster Bay in 1933. When he later learned that *Vamarie* had won a race from Miami to Nassau in weather so heavy it had caused nine of the twelve entrants to retire, he became an enthusiast for wishbones.

It was not an easy gestation. Uffa was used to dealing with his own small team of craftsmen aboard the Floating Bridge, not the many layers of management found within a large shipyard more used to naval destroyers than gentlemen's yachts. Because Uffa was impulsive, short-tempered and impatient, conflicts quickly built up within the team that White's had created for the *Wishbone* project. He often swore like a bargee, and even laced his dispatches with expletives and criticisms of the workforce. Unsurprisingly, this caused offence, and White's head of correspondence had to carefully censor long sections of his instructions before they could be distributed.

One of White's secretaries was designated to work with Uffa at the Floating Bridge and take dictation from him (he dictated everything), but she soon resigned, and in the end he employed a male secretary, Charles Willis. By then it was clear that only a man (and a steady one at that) would put up with his tantrums and foul language. Willis was an efficient worker and managed to impose a sense of order in Uffa's

---

121   A wishbone gaff is a spar that connects the two masts of a ketch, thereby strengthening them and increasing the sail area with only a small penalty in additional weight.

otherwise chaotic administration. In particular, he made sure that Uffa completed, on time, the books he had promised to Peter Davies (one new book per year). Willis was also the only person who was able to talk Uffa out of his wilder ideas, and the two men found a *modus operandi* that allowed both the business and the writing to get done. The boatyard rarely made a profit, but its finances would have been in a much worse state had the pragmatic Willis not taken a firm hand with them.

Uffa's mood swings were intense and, at times, so black that he would disappear for days on end. He may have suffered from what we now call bipolar disorder—then known as manic depression. When on a high, he had phenomenal energy and effervesced with ideas, but when down he could hardly function as a businessman at all. Today, this lifelong condition is treatable with drugs and counselling, but there was no reliable remedy at that time, and it was not, anyway, in Uffa's nature to seek help.

Wishbone was finished on time and with great ceremony, but other projects had been delayed (he rarely turned new orders down) and Uffa was forced to sell iron structures from the Floating Bridge as scrap metal to pay his men's wages. He often gave his customers novel excuses when their boats did not arrive on time. Isaac 'Ikey' Bell[122] had commissioned a tender for his racing yacht, *Bloodhound*,[123] which was being built by Nicholson's. When he complained to Uffa of late delivery, he got the reply, 'I cannot build the thing because I am disturbed so much at night by the singing of the nightingales.'

Ikey sent a telegram by return, 'Shoot the bloody birds and build the boat in your own good time. Ikey.' Uffa

---

122   Isaac 'Ikey' Bell, was a wealthy American sportsman who'd settled in Ireland to pursue his two passions: riding to hounds in winter and yacht racing in summer.
123   *Bloodhound* was bought by the royal family in 1962 and used as a cruiser which would occasionally race. She was often carried abord the royal yacht *Britannia*.

"WISHBONE."

AUX. KETCH RIGGED STEEL YACHT.

PRINCIPAL DIMENSIONS :-

Length, overall	...	...	83' 0"
Do. waterline	...	...	60' 0"
Beam	...	...	17' 4"
Depth, admidships	...	...	13'10"
Draught extreme	...	...	10' 0"
Displacement	...	...	60 tons.
Weight of lead keel	...	...	25 tons.
Sail Area	...	...	3,000 sq. ft.

Built under Lloyds Special Survey for 100 A.1. Class.

The yacht is built of mild steel, and is electric welded throughout, no rivets being used, and is the first ocean cruiser to be so constructed.

Launch of the all electrically welded Yacht

"WISHBONE."

By THE HON. MRS. ALAN COLMAN,

Built by MESSRS. J. SAMUEL WHITE & COMPANY, L⟨

for ALAN COLMAN, Esq.

Designed by UFFA FOX, Esq.

Cowes, I.W.   1st June

And see ! She stirs !

She starts—she moves—she seems to feel

The thrill of life along her keel

And spurning with her foot the ground

With one exulting, joyous bound,

She leaps into the Ocean's arms !

And lo ! from the assembled crowd

There rose a shout prolonged and loud

That to the ocean seemed to say—

" Take her, O Bridegroom, old and grey

Take her to thy protecting arms,

With all her youth and all her charms."

Longfellow.

𝕸enu.

WISHBONE SOUP.

ALL WELDED LOBSTER (without) RIVET S⟨

DUCKLING a là COLMAN (always alive⟩

GREEN PEAS a là UFFA FOX (not too gre⟨

NEW GAFF POTATOES.

CREME ALL WHITE a là COWES.

PROGRESS CHEESE.

treasured the reply and prioritised the tender which Ikey was delighted with.

In 2006, the Norfolk-based yacht skipper, Ernie Vince, fondly remembered his time on *Wishbone*: 'Then [a friend] contacted me one day. He was very friendly with the Colman family—the mustard people. Mr Alan in particular. And he said, "I've had Mr Alan Colman on to me. His Scotch skipper has left him, and he's got no one for the season. Would you be interested?" So I said, "Oh yes." So instead, I took the schooner (sic)—*Wishbone*—Mr Colman's yacht and fitted out at his own berth and boat-building shops on the Broads.

'We went all over the place with her, she was a lovely thing. She was a beautiful thing to sail, a gaff rig schooner (sic).[124] She was actually the first all-welded British steel yacht. The very first one that was all welded steel. She was very fast.

'… I took the yacht up to Stockholm, and he [Alan Colman] flew out to Stockholm and joined us, and then we cruised about the Gulf of Finland. We got as far as Kotka, which is a very big timber port on the Finnish/Russian border. And on this particular day at Kotka, he said, "Tomorrow, if everything's all right, we'll sail up the last few miles up to Petrograd."

'So off they went ashore on their day's sightseeing, and he said, "We'll be back about five." But at midday, one of the chaps was on deck and called out, "The Guv'nor is on the quay, waving like the devil." So I said, "All right. Well, get the launch and go and get him." So they packed him off aboard. He said, "Ernie, war is imminent." He said, "We're advised to get back to England as quickly as we can." So he said, "I've booked a flight from Helsinki. You get underway as quickly as you can, and get back."

'We got back to Lowestoft at midnight on the Thursday, and war was declared on the Sunday morning. All the time we were

---

124   *Wishbone*'s mizzen mast was shorter than her main mast, meaning that she was really a ketch, but she was often referred to as a schooner.

going out to the Skaggerack and so on, there was loads of big German trawlers going out, obviously all off out minelaying somewhere. Anyhow, we escaped that all right—just.'[125]

The Uffa Fox–designed, welded-steel ketch, *Wishbone* in 1935.

125   Thompson, Paul. *Sea-Change—Wivenhoe Remembered.* The History Press. 2006.

Chapter 8
Twenty Acres

Uffa had outgrown the Floating Bridge and needed to find a new home. His burgeoning fame (he now broadcast regularly—if uncomfortably—on the BBC), and the fact that the Floating Bridge was so accessible, led to a steady stream of visitors and there were too many interruptions for his and Alma's taste. Since 1914, Samuel Saunders (Uffa's first employer) had owned and lived in Padmore House, which occupied a substantial estate stretching from Whippingham to the Folly. Saunders died in 1933, at the age of seventy-six, and his son, Hubert, broke up the estate, putting several parcels of land up for sale.[126] Uffa grasped the opportunity and bought twenty acres on the east bank of the Medina River between the Folly Inn and the Old East Medina Mill. 'I naturally bought the land adjoining the river with a quarter of a mile of river frontage on its western boundary. To the south its border was a clean, clear, ever-running, freshwater stream, while to the north it was bounded by a wood. A rookery formed its eastern boundary. The ground sloped towards the south and west and caught sunshine all day, the two woods shielded the property from the cold north and east winds, a warm, cosy corner of the island I have always loved.'[127]

Buying such a large plot meant that he would have space to hunt, shoot and observe nature while being sufficiently off

126   Mills, A D. *The Place-Names of the Isle of Wight*. Paul Watkins Publishing. 1966.
127   Fox, Uffa. *Joys of Life*. Newnes. 1966.

the beaten track to avoid uninvited guests. The new house would be sited at the end of a long drive and could not be seen from any public road. Another man would have hired an architect and a builder, but Uffa set about designing his new home himself. Much of the work would be done by his own craftsmen, leading to even longer delays in boat deliveries and more pressure on his cash flow but, once a new idea had taken root, it took priority over all other things. Throughout his life he would design, build, or extensively rebuild his homes and workshops. Architecture interested him almost as much as boatbuilding and he knew exactly what he wanted. He set high standards, and when one of his builders pointed out that the foundations formed a raft that would float a cinema, Uffa warned: 'I don't mind this house sliding down into the river on this clay soil, but when it arrives, I don't want to see a crack in any of its walls or corners.'[128]

Like a yacht, the rooms would be exquisitely panelled in oak, mahogany and teak. Rainwater would be gathered from the roof and there was no gas or electricity. 'Although these two services may be great boons and benefits of our time, houses spring up like weeds once water and electricity are at hand.'[129] When the local authority wrote to him asking where his water supply came from, Uffa replied: 'The good Lord supplies my needs.' One of the paradoxes that defined Uffa was his mistrust of twentieth-century technology, despite having made his name from the cutting-edge fluid dynamics he had learned at Saunders—itself the result of rapid advances made during World War I. Uffa feared that automation (then a popular buzzword) would herald a new Dark Age. In his autobiography he wrote, 'Our masters, the machines, will be tended by a few men working three days of twelve hours each … This prospect of our future is no idle dream. Its shadow is already falling across the lives of a generation which, perhaps

---

128   Fox, Uffa. *Joys of Life*. Newnes. 1966.
129   Ibid.

Uffa at Twenty Acres, the house he designed and built for himself. Image courtesy of Mike Dixon.

through no fault of its own, does not even know what a full life can mean.'[130]

He acquired a twenty-four-seat dining table—which bore Queen Victoria's seal—from Osborne House, and his dining room was literally built around it. There was a substantial library and a spacious well-lit drawing office. He also had boathouses and slipways built at the river's edge, so he always had easy access to his beloved Medina.

The house would, in time, become almost a museum, as Uffa had collected and treasured so many *objets d'art*, often

130   Fox, Uffa. *Joys of Life*. Newnes. 1966.

with royal or artistic provenance. They included Prince Henry of Battenburg's twelve-bore gun, the pillars from Handel's organ, Lord Byron's piano and J M Barrie's bible box, which Uffa used to conceal his telephone (telephony was one of his few concessions to twentieth-century technology).[131] He called his new home, simply, Twenty Acres.

Uffa disingenuously described himself as a '… naturally easy-going sort of chap who disliked arguments'. In truth, he thrived on quarrels—especially with the authorities—and went to great lengths to win them. He delighted in outwitting officials of any sort and celebrated his triumphs with as much pride as his victories in yacht races. During the war, when he wanted to store one of his lifeboats in the hangar of a US Air Force base, his friend, Weston Martyr, warned him that if he as much as approached the airfield without permission, he risked being shot by the military police. Uffa not only found a way in, but also charmed the commanding officer so completely that the Americans wined and dined him while organising an impromptu flying display for his entertainment. On the same trip Martyr assured Uffa that the local Observer Corps base had such strict security that Churchill himself could not enter without the right paperwork. Uffa saw this as a challenge and tried to get in via a half-open canteen window. He was caught and the police were called, but when the head of the unit recognised Uffa (he owned one of his boats, *The Vixen*, and had won all the local races in the 1925 season) he called off the police and took him to lunch.

When bicycles were ridden over his footpaths—churning up the clay soil and destroying the grass—he installed stiles, but the cyclists quickly dismantled them. Uffa responded by firing both barrels of his shotgun through the front wheel of an obstinate cyclist, claiming that he was aiming at a rabbit. The cyclist threatened court action, but never carried it out and no cyclist went near to Uffa's land for many years.

---

131   Dixon, June; *UFFA FOX: A Personal Biography*, Angus & Robertson, 1978.

Twenty Acres

Not long after the house was completed a power-generating station was built at nearby Kingston. The council wanted to use compulsory purchase orders to run high tension cables across his land, but Uffa outwitted them. He invited officials to his house for sherry, and surreptitiously copied their plans to be sure of the exact locations of the pylons. He then lodged plans of his own to build outbuildings in those precise locations. At that time, a landowner did not need special planning consent to put up dwellings on their own land. When the authorities saw Uffa's plans, they realised that they had been hoodwinked, and their pylons would have to make a detour of Uffa's twenty acres or go under them. In the end, at huge expense, they went under.

Uffa allowed much of his land to remain unspoilt and uncultivated, as he liked to use his estate for shooting, rambling and boating with his friends, especially as he had permission to shoot on most of the neighbouring farms. Once settled at Twenty Acres, he acquired a cook, butler and chauffeur and began to live as if he were a country squire. Much as it suited his personality, he could never really afford such a grand lifestyle and the cost of it would add considerably to his financial woes. Nevertheless, he would remember his days at Twenty Acres as among his happiest.

His new home finished, Uffa, who was then in his late thirties, decided it was time to learn to drive. In his writing he often condemned cars as a noisome twentieth-century technology that blighted the countryside and caused fatal accidents. As a driver, however, his relationship with automobiles was closer to that of Toad in Kenneth Graham's *The Wind in the Willows*.[132] He owned many cars at once, crashed them frequently and largely ignored the laws that applied to them. Uffa was a superb

---

132   Toad of Toad Hall, having crashed all eight of his cars, was arrested, tried, and found guilty of offences including driving recklessly, and insulting a police officer (Uffa would often face similar charges). In Toad's case the verdict was guilty, and he was sentenced to 20 years' imprisonment. Uffa was usually acquitted.

helmsman who could squeeze every last knot of speed from any boat under sail. Unfortunately, he drove cars the same way, with his right foot firmly to the floor.

He began with a second-hand Morris which he drove frantically around his own estate until he felt confident enough to go out onto public roads. Until 1935, you did not need to take a driving test in Britain, and most people simply taught themselves by trial and error. Driving under the influence of alcohol did not become an offence until 1967, and Uffa saw no harm in having a fortifying drink or two before getting behind the wheel or, for that matter, the helm. King Charles, who as a boy sailed with Uffa and Prince Philip, recalls, 'I remember when I was about ten years old, Uffa used to say, "Now come on, you've got to drink two glasses of champagne before you go out racing".'[133]

The Isle of Wight's roads, then and now, tend to be narrow, twisting, and the hedgerows make it difficult to see ahead. This did not prevent Uffa from driving everywhere as fast as the car could go. Many passengers, having once experienced his driving, would refuse to go out with him again, and those who persevered learnt not to try and apply imaginary brakes from the passenger seat. Uffa especially disliked this and would scold anyone whose foot hit the floor when he approached a bend. He even had the passenger seat adjusted so that if your foot pressed down hard enough the seat was released, and you were tipped into the back of the car. Finally, he had a bizarre dial mounted on the dashboard which registered tons of pressure and could be activated by a harmonium foot pedal installed on the driver's side. If a passenger asked what the gauge was for, Uffa would reply, 'It's all the energy you are wasting by putting your foot on the brake.'

Uffa loved to wine and dine his friends and was a wonderful host. Owning Twenty Acres allowed him to entertain on a scale which would have been impossible on the Floating

---

133   Kerley, Lisa. *Memories of the Sea—Interview with Tony Dixon*, 9th August 2018.

Bridge. On his own estate, and with servants, he could regale his guests like a mediaeval baron, and often did so. There were many memorable dinners and afterwards, much fortified by good wine and port, he liked to take his guests out for a little night shooting. Rabbits are easily mesmerised by car headlamps so, at two o'clock one morning, Uffa loaded his guests into his large American car and drove off with the sunroof open and headlamps blazing. One friend stood on the seat beside him with his head out of the roof and another sat on the roof itself with his legs dangling inside. Each held a twelve-bore shotgun which they fired at every rabbit they saw. One of Uffa's fields had recently been ploughed, but this did not prevent him from driving flat out across it as his friends blazed away. The rabbits scattered *en masse* and Uffa hotly pursued them.

When a twenty-foot-wide blackberry bush appeared in front of the car, Uffa drove straight through it at thirty miles an hour. His friend on the roof was swept away by the brambles, and his other friend, standing on the seat, was flattened across the roof with his gun torn from his hands. Although scratched and bleeding, Uffa got them back on board, found their guns, and set off again in pursuit of the rabbits. As he drove beneath the low branches of an oak tree, the same thing happened again but, once more, he recovered his friends with their guns and continued. Between them they had bagged nothing and were, by now, running short of cartridges. Uffa continued to drive pell-mell and as fast as he could towards any rabbit they saw. When one of his new five-barred gates appeared, he drove straight through it, instantly turning it into matchsticks. At four o'clock the car finally gave up and they walked back to the house. A local garage recovered the vehicle the next day—it had broken its half shafts and the clutch was completely burned out.

Throughout his life Uffa would have adventures involving cars. In the middle of World War II, when British cities were being heavily bombed, Uffa arrived in London to collect two engines for the Airborne Lifeboats he was then building in Cowes. The two right-hand doors of his car were missing, following a collision with an army lorry, and he had ignored several road signs, gone through a red light and made an illegal right turn. He always ignored traffic lights and road signs in London because, he said, there were no such gadgets on the Isle of Wight and there were, consequently, no traffic problems!

Having collected his engines, he parked outside the Hyde Park Hotel in his usual manner—with two wheels on and two wheels off the pavement. When he came back a policeman was waiting for him. During the war it was law that cars had to be left locked, but the missing doors made this impossible. The policeman also noted that the tax disc had expired (Uffa then owned six cars and hadn't bothered to renew the tax on any of them). Furthermore, he was not carrying an ID card (also illegal during the war) and when the policeman looked at an expensive overcoat on the back seat, he saw a label that read 'Leonard P Mew Esq.' Uffa was, however, carrying a driving licence, but that had also expired. He explained that his Cowes home had been bombed and his friend, Lenny Mew, had lent him some clothes. When the policeman finally let him go, Uffa drove straight down Knightsbridge and then—in the constable's full view—went through another red light while making an illegal right turn. A lengthy report was sent to the Cowes police, but they knew Uffa well and decided (not for the first or last time) that in the middle of a war they had more important things to worry about.

On another occasion, Uffa was driving furiously past the Albany Barracks in Newport, when a military policeman on traffic duty signalled him to stop to allow troops to cross the road. Uffa, as usual, ignored him and sped past. The army reported Uffa to the Cowes Police, one of whom quipped that if he had been driving at his normal speed they wouldn't have read his number in the first place. Nevertheless, Uffa was summoned to appear at the Magistrates' Court where he represented himself (during the war, troops had a legal right to stop the traffic). Lawyers have a saying that the man who represents himself has a fool for a client, but Uffa's line of questioning would have done credit to the finest king's councillor in the land.

Two soldiers were called as witnesses and Uffa chose to question only one, reasoning—inexplicably—that a red-headed man would be easier to examine than one with brown hair. When Uffa began to make a statement, the magistrate interjected, 'You cannot say anything unless you go in the witness box'. But Uffa continued all the same.

'I wish to state that these questions are not to disprove anything these two men have said, for I am certain both are speaking the truth.'

The magistrate was plainly relieved and smiled as Uffa asked the ginger-headed soldier: 'Was I on a main road?'

'Yes.'

'Was there any need for me to stop for traffic on this clear main road?'

'No.'

'Was there any accident of any kind?'

'No.'

'Is it correct procedure to give minor roads precedence over major roads?'

'Well ... I suppose it is not strictly correct. I did not think of it that way.'

'Were these men coming off a private road on to a main road?'

'Yes.'

'Do you agree that the Army chose khaki because it is an invisible colour?'

'I do not agree. The Army chose khaki because you cannot see it.' There was laughter which was silenced by the bench.

'Was the soldier signalling, as well as wearing khaki uniform, also wearing khaki gloves?'

'Of course he was in this wintry weather.'

'Does a military policeman on point duty controlling traffic wear white armlets?'

'Yes.'

'Did this military policeman have white armlets on?'

'No.'

'Do men who are controlling traffic past a steam roller have flags?'

'Yes.'

'Does the Army use flags to signal one another?'

'Yes.'

'Did this man use flags?'

'No.'

'What colour are the trees at this time of the year?'

'A brown colour,' then pointing to his uniform, 'almost this colour.'

There were more giggles as the bench retired and shortly delivered a verdict of case dismissed. Uffa took the two soldiers into the nearby Wheatsheaf where they had, what he later described as, a 'merry midday meal'. The Isle of Wight *County Press* recorded the proceedings under the headline, *The Invisible Man.*

Late one evening, when Uffa was playing cards with friends in Blackwater, just south of Newport, a policeman knocked at the door and demanded to know who owned the car that had been parked across the level crossing, stopping the train in its tracks. This time, Uffa pleaded guilty but added, in mitigation, 'That damned train has kept me waiting often enough.'[134]

In the 1950s Uffa was driving his huge Packard car from Puckaster to Cowes after a recent shower had left standing water on the road. As usual, he was going very fast. He

---

134   https://www.islandlifemagazine.co.uk/uffa-fox-boat-designer-and-much-more

skidded off the road and over a bank, then over a ditch and finally through a hedge. The car was so badly damaged that it took a month to repair, and Uffa received a deep cut above his eyebrow, which bled profusely. Just as he got to his house the doctor of Parkhurst prison telephoned to talk about the cricket match on the Brambles the following day. 'When I told him what had happened, he jumped in his car, was soon with me, and after we had both enjoyed a couple of gins and tonics, he cleaned the wound in my head and stitched it up.'

Uffa was always a passionate cricketer and after the war he began the tradition, still observed, of the Brambles cricket match. During the autumn equinox there will usually be a few days when the Bramble Bank, halfway across the Solent, is dry. The day after he had been stitched up by Dr Brian Pollock of Parkhurst Prison, Uffa took thirty cricketers out to the Bramble on his twenty-ton cutter, *Fresh Breeze*. Uffa's team played a team from Parkhurst Prison, captained by the Governor. Uffa won the toss and batted first. His team won the match narrowly, possibly because any ball that landed in the water counted as a six, and the tide was rapidly coming in! In fact, it was lapping at their feet when they finally gathered the stumps and their Red Ensign and sailed back to Cowes.

Throughout his life, Uffa had sung, and knew the lyrics of many songs by heart, including a remarkable number of traditional sea shanties. While sailing together on his schooner, *Lumberjack*, and hearing Uffa sing through the night, Max Aitken suggested Uffa should record them, warning that they might be permanently lost if he did not. Years later, the composer and conductor Ron Goodwin, along with the record producer George Martin (of Beatles fame), arrived in Cowes to hear Uffa. As the ferry that brought them from the mainland steamed past the Commodore's House, Uffa fired a salute from the brass cannon he kept on the roof. Unfortunately, he overcharged it, and had to greet the two men with features that looked like 'spotted dick', swabbing his face with a bloody towel.

Uffa was later recorded by Goodwin and Martin in London, supported by twenty musicians and the Mike Sammes Singers, a well-known vocal ensemble of the day. Unusually, Uffa introduces each song in his speaking voice. Thanks to his bronchitis, his fine treble voice was not what it had once been but, nonetheless, the resulting record, *Uffa Sings Sea Shanties*, was well received by critics and became a modest hit with the public. Uffa even performed the shanties for Winston Churchill at the eighty-second birthday party of Lord Beaverbrook. The evening was a success with Churchill enthusiastically conducting, using his huge cigar as a baton. Uffa loved to perform in public, but later turned down an invitation to appear on stage as a shanty-singing comedian.

There had once been a famous regatta at the Folly and there had long been talk of reviving it. At precisely six o'clock one evening (opening time), twenty-three men, led by Uffa, George Barton and Lennie Mew, arrived at the Folly Inn and put the idea to the publican, Bob Savage.[135] Lennie proposed Uffa as President, and he agreed on three conditions:

1) That a committee of thirty be formed, composed of ten small committees each composed of three men (there was no suggestion that women might be involved), and each committee would deal with a single aspect of the regatta. Uffa would be available for advice but not to vote.

---

135   Lennie Mew was a scion of the Isle of Wight brewers, Mew and Langton, whose 'Royal Brewery' stood at the junction of Crocker Street and Holyrood Street in Newport. In 1965, the company was sold to Strong and Co (later Whitbread), who were only interested in Mew and Langton's 144 pubs. The old brewery building was acquired by the Isle of White Council, who left it empty until 1979 when it was severely damaged by fire. The burned-out shell remains empty and derelict to this day.

UFFA SINGS

mono

PARLOPHONE

SEA SHANTIES
AND JACK ASHORE SONGS

ORCHESTRA AND CHORUS
DIRECTED BY
RON GOODWIN

2) Each man would contribute one guinea to the regatta's funds.

3) That each man drink a pint before he left

Uffa recalled, 'This was joyfully agreed, so I ordered twenty-three pints of beer and we soon wrapped ourselves round our first pint and felt much the better for it.'

Lennie and the others had been wise to allow Uffa to run the committee on his own terms. They knew that he could be incredibly productive when given a free hand, but impossible if opposed by others. It didn't matter that he had no vote, because he would inevitably get his own way whatever happened. His reputation, contacts and influence in the sailing world were such that it was better to have him working with them than against them, so everyone agreed and enjoyed several more pints. 'By the end of the evening we were very mellow, and felt that if we tilted our head sideways, beer would run out of our ears.' So mellow, in fact, that when the Folly Inn closed, they went to Lennie Mew's house in the Royal Brewery and went on drinking until five o'clock the following morning.

As well as many races for small boats of all classes, there were fun events, including a barrel of beer tied to a pole to be won by the first boat to retrieve it. 'The innocent thought they only had to win the rowing part of the race and arrive first to get the barrel, but it was well and truly lashed, and as the swift, early innocent oarsmen tried to undo, and then cut through the cords with a knife, the rest arrived. As we had lashed the barrel very skilfully, we knew that before it came down every boat in the race would be on the spot jostling and bustling each other before the beer came down. Soon the river was full of sunken boats, swimming men, oars, and paddles floating all over the place, till finally all in the race swam ashore with the barrel between them and shared it out among themselves. Meanwhile their sunken boats and gear floated all over the river. For all knew that the beer would soon go, but their boats would stay as it was high-water slack.'[136]

The Folly Regatta was a great success and ran until the 1990s, outliving the men who revived it. When Bob Savage retired, Uffa's niece, Lucy, and her husband John McQueen Mason, took over both the Inn and the Regatta. Rodney Barton (George Barton's son) recalls, 'I was Chairman when we reluctantly made the decision to abandon the event. It was the cost of insurance, lack of big yachts taking part, and health and safety regulations. East Cowes Sailing Club is the custodian of the trophies.'

Uffa's business was growing—he now built more than

---

136   Fox, Uffa. *Joys of Life*. Newnes. 1966.

thirty bespoke boats per year. When he outgrew the Floating Bridge he bought an old pub, the Trinity Arms in East Cowes, and used that as a workshop but it too became insufficient. As well as fourteen-foot dinghies he also designed and built larger displacement boats, and the search for bigger premises became urgent. He needed a larger work area, wider slipways and deeper water, and he found those at the Medina Yard in Birmingham Road, West Cowes. He now purchased the substantial riverside property along with Medina House (and later, in 1942, the next-door Westbourne House) which had originally been Birmingham Hall.[137] Uffa converted Medina House into a home with fine views across the Solent, as well as generously proportioned drawing and other offices. He purchased the old king-pin roof which had once sat above Trinity Wharf at East Cowes and re-erected it above Medina Yard so that he could enjoy uninterrupted views across the river, the sea and a large part of the Island. As usual, he would live directly above his workplace and waste no time commuting. The shipyard was extensively converted, with workshops and a new slipway added. Uffa could now easily build anything from a dinghy up to a vessel of twelve metres and he doubted that racing yachts would ever get bigger. 'Medina House and Yard brought me great happiness. It was always a joy to walk round, as it was so compact and efficient. Timber came in one end at the sawmills, straight on to the saw benches, and was launched at the other end as a swift and lovely vessel … all our days in Medina Yard were very happy.'

---

137   Westbourne House was the birthplace of the educator Thomas Arnold (1795–1842) and is today, once more, a private home. The next-door Medina House was damaged by bombs during the Blitz but rebuilt after the war. It was later demolished, and the site is now occupied by the Tides Reach residential complex.

Uffa Fox on the slipway at Medina Yard.
Image courtesy of Mike Dixon.

Chapter Nine
The Airborne Lifeboat

Uffa fell in love easily and passionately. Once he identified something he wanted, it was in his nature to move heaven and earth to gain it, irrespective of the cost. Consequently, he had several affairs outside his marriage. Alma knew about most of them—he was indiscreet and one of his mistresses had even left personal items in the bedroom at Twenty Acres—but whatever Alma may have felt, she remained with Uffa and, generally, waited for the affairs to blow over.

Uffa had close friends across the social spectrum, he was as comfortable with working men as he was with royalty, and he enjoyed all kinds of company. Lord Ruthven, Peter Davies' father-in-law, was fond of Uffa and often entertained him at his Bembridge home. At one soirée, he introduced him to Mrs Laura Louisa Enoch, better known as Cherry. She was the widow of a diplomat, who kept a guesthouse near to Ruthven's home. Uffa was immediately taken by her; she was intelligent, vivacious, and, most importantly, had a curvaceous figure—he was never attracted to slim women ('their legs are like canaries'). The first time they dined together at her home, he suggested they take a walk on the beach to 'settle the digestion'. It was a pleasant evening and he said, 'fine night for a swim,' before throwing off all his clothes and diving naked into the sea. Cherry quickly learned that he was nothing if not impulsive.

Uffa rented a remote cottage with no telephone near to Quarr Abbey. Ostensibly, it was a writer's retreat where he could work on his books without interruption—he claimed that Twenty Acres was too busy and there were too many distractions—but the cottage now became a love nest, where he could discreetly meet Cherry. Caution, however, was not part of his make-up, and the affair was soon public knowledge. On New Year's Eve, 1938, Uffa invited Cherry to Twenty Acres to celebrate the festivities with his friends and family. By now, Alma had guessed, or heard, that Cherry was his mistress but, as before, she let him have his way, assuming it would quickly blow over. As midnight approached, Uffa suggested Cherry accompany him while he walked the dogs in his grounds. Alma watched from an upstairs window and saw, despite the darkness, the couple making love. Whether this was simply over-exuberance on their part, or whether they intended to be seen, is impossible to say, but it was too much—even for the patient Alma—and she packed her bags and left.

Uffa—always the optimist—assumed that the separation was temporary, and moved his younger sister, Ellie, along with his nephew, Peter Dixon, and his father, Arthur, into Twenty Acres to help him keep house while waiting for Alma to return. The days, however, turned into weeks, then months, and Uffa finally had to accept that her departure was permanent. Although they would remain friends, and Uffa would later try to be reconciled with her, the long-suffering Alma was steadfast and never returned to him. She did, however, agree to an amicable divorce which left Uffa's chaotic finances intact and enabled him to marry Cherry, with Uffa's long-standing friend, Sir Peter Scott, as best man. There was no time for a honeymoon, as Uffa's restless spirit was already preoccupied with a burning new idea.

By maintaining homes at Twenty Acres and Medina House,

Uffa had few inhibitions: 'Modesty is only a sense of physical imperfection.' Image courtesy of Mike Dixon.

Uffa was, as usual, stretching his income to breaking point and he continued to lurch from one financial crisis to another as a lengthening chain of creditors arrived at his door. In marked contrast, his father, Arthur, was careful with money and moderately wealthy, owning a significant property portfolio. Arthur had lent to Uffa many times and was adamant that he would advance no more, but Uffa's problems were pressing, and he could be very persuasive when in a corner. 'You're not getting another penny out of me!' was Arthur's constant response, but Uffa wore him down.

Uffa proposed that a company, Uffa Fox Ltd, be formed into which he would put all his business assets and Arthur would put the bulk of his remaining capital. Arthur reluctantly agreed on the express proviso that Ellie, who suffered from poor health, be given a permanent home and that Uffa would swear to always look after her. This was one of the few promises to his father that Uffa faithfully kept, protecting his sister for the rest of her life.

Uffa had the political foresight to see, from a long way off, that a second war was coming, even when others dismissed the idea. He knew from his experience of World War I that private yacht building would stop as all materials would be needed for the war effort, but there would be government contracts for those able to fulfil them. His mind turned to what his yard might be able to produce in wartime. At first, he had little success, but he eventually gained a sub-contract from another Island company to make pontoons for the Ministry of Supply. Cherry's finances were little better than his, her guest house was losing money and attracted few guests. Uffa moved her into an apartment in Medina House along with her son, Bobbie Sach. Although Uffa had always said he wanted no children, he became firm friends with the young boy, teaching him to sail along with the rudiments of boatbuilding. In time Bobbie became one of Uffa's apprentices.

When Uffa learned that his sixteen-year-old niece, June

Dixon, had passed her exams in shorthand and typing, he immediately offered her work as a secretary. He dictated all of his correspondence, all of his books, and expected his staff to attend to all the administration and paperwork. While many of his secretaries found him difficult and soon left, June was quietly efficient and stayed with him for many years.[138]

June arrived in time to witness Uffa's first and only strike. For all his eccentricities, he generally bonded well with his men and often lent them the money to buy their houses. Consequently, they were, on the whole, loyal and hardworking—many of them would work for Uffa for almost their entire careers. Uffa's temper, however, was fearsome and his foul-mouthed tirades could be heard several streets away. One worker shouted back, accusing Uffa of having mistreated his first wife, Alma. Uffa fired him, told June to type a carefully worded notice of dismissal, and personally delivered it to the man's home on a Sunday. The union, however, invoked an ancient law which prohibited dismissal on a Sunday, and demanded that he be reinstated. When Uffa refused, the union called out his men on strike, and only the apprentices, fitters and draughtsmen remained at work. Uffa wrote on his calendar, 'This is one of the saddest and unhappiest days of my life.'

In normal times, the strike would have brought his boatyard to its knees, but these were not normal times. The pontoon work he was doing was less demanding than boatbuilding and did not require the same level of skill and craftsmanship. Uffa was able to hire non-union labour without a serious delay, and his yard reopened within a week. He also invested in new machinery and was soon fully operational again. None of the striking men were taken back and Uffa moved on with little difficulty.

---

138   June Dixon was the daughter of Uffa's older sister, Mahala. She would later record her experiences in *UFFA FOX—A Personal Biography*, which was published in 1978, a few years after Uffa's death.

New staff meant improvements to the facilities and another of Uffa's fixations came into play. Like the Romans, he thought that defecation was a group activity and a good opportunity for conversation. He installed new open-plan lavatories with no doors or cubicles and was baffled when his men refused to use them. If he called meetings in the new toilets, his men would turn up and stand expectantly with notebooks in hand but refused to join Uffa in the way he intended. He had always been uninhibited about public nudity and bodily functions but was bemused by the reticence of others. When he installed a bidet in the bathroom of Medina House, it became an object of wonder for those who visited in his absence. Safe in the knowledge that Uffa was away for the day, groups of apprentices and others would literally stand in awe of the contraption, which was covered by a tablecloth and a vase of flowers. One curious apprentice turned on the taps and a spray of water hit the ceiling. Uffa was later heard to complain that his bathroom had sprung a leak. Many years passed before the guilty party admitted to Uffa what had really happened, and they both roared with laughter.

Although Medina Yard was, by and large, a disciplined workplace, there could be respites for the workforce if one of Uffa's many passions seized him. When a nearby lake froze (a rare occurrence on the temperate Isle of Wight) he took the boys skating, and soon organised them into impromptu ice hockey teams. The games were so chaotic, and there were so many pratfalls and so much laughter, that afterwards no one could remember who had actually won.

Bobbie Sach, Uffa's stepson, became the first of the apprentices to volunteer for military service during the war. He wanted to join the Royal Air Force's Air-Sea Rescue Branch and was delighted when they accepted him. At the beginning of World War II, Air-Sea Rescue hardly existed, and aircrew who bailed out over the sea had barely one chance in five of being saved alive. Adrift in rubber dinghies, the prevailing winds often blew them onto an enemy coast where they were captured. Worse still, long exposure to cold and damp frequently caused them to lose their limbs, if not their lives, even when rescued. While at home on leave, the young Bobbie explained to Uffa the huge problems involved in rescuing aircrew from the sea. It was precisely the kind of challenge Uffa thrived upon, and the many difficulties that had to be overcome simply sent his fertile mind into overdrive. Before long, he and Bill Waight, his old friend and chief draughtsman, were exchanging ideas.

In 1941, a telegram arrived with the terrible news that Bobbie had been posted as 'Missing in Action.' Both Cherry and Uffa were devastated and long, painful days followed until they were told that he was alive. Bobbie's boat (as frequently happened) had gone close to the French coast to try and rescue a downed pilot, but they had been attacked and captured by a German patrol boat. Bobbie was seriously injured and spent many weeks in hospital before being sent to a prisoner of war camp in Germany where he would remain for the duration of the war. His internment was a constant, nagging reminder to Uffa of the urgency of Air-Sea Rescue.

As the war intensified, the Isle of Wight would, itself, become a target. Cowes, at the mouth of the distinctive Medina River, was an easy town for German pilots to find as they crossed the Channel from Northern France, and the Island became a target of opportunity for pilots unable, or unwilling, to fly over the mainland. The shipyards of J S White and others, along with the hangars of Saunders-Roe, were regularly attacked. Uffa sent his men on aircraft recognition courses and posted them on the roof of Medina House with a klaxon horn, to warn of approaching bombers. They were so dependable that Cowes residents learned to ignore the official sirens and only respond to Uffa's klaxon.

Uffa volunteered for the Local Defence Volunteers (later the Home Guard) and, at the same time, volunteered his entire workforce, ignoring the inconvenient fact that many had already volunteered as air raid wardens, firemen, etc. At the same time, he dismissed two men who claimed to be conscientious objectors. One explained that he couldn't kill because he was a Christian. 'What do you think I am?' fumed Uffa, 'A bloody heathen?'[139] The other man wrote to his MP to complain, but Uffa ignored the letters which followed, and nothing further happened.

Uffa, naturally, took command of the Medina Yard Home Guard Unit, which he nicknamed the Uffashots. He was given the rank of lieutenant, but soon began to agitate for promotion to captain. As well as the yard, they were expected to protect the police station, the grocer's shop and the Duke of York pub (this was Uffa's local and Harry Wingham, the licensee, was quickly made a sergeant in Uffa's unit). They rarely drilled and wore such a hotchpotch of uniforms that June Dixon recalled, 'They made *Dad's Army* look like a crack Guards regiment.'[140]

Uffa managed to acquire a machine gun salvaged from a German aircraft which force-landed on the Island. He mounted it on a makeshift gantry on top of his car, which he could access through the sunroof. The long-suffering Cowes police knew Uffa well, and usually turned a blind eye to his many eccentricities. This time, however, there were so many complaints from the public that they had to intervene, and the gun was removed. Nevertheless, it soon became clear that Uffa had succeeded—where armourers from the Woolwich Arsenal had failed—in adapting German guns for British use. Consequently, Uffa was usually first on the scene when a German plane was shot down over the Island, and he was allowed to remove the guns and ammunition, half of which he kept. Before long, Uffa's Home Guard unit was the best armed and equipped on the Island, largely with enemy weapons!

---

139   Dixon, June, *UFFA FOX: A Personal Biography*, Angus & Robertson, 1978.
140   Ibid.

Uffa commanded the Medina Yard Home Guard Unit,
which he nicknamed the Uffashots.

If firefighting duty coincided with guard duty, Uffa always juggled the two so that one became an excuse for not fulfilling the other. After a couple of hours of either duty, Uffa and his men generally decamped to the Duke of York, where they remained until closing time. From time to time army units would 'attack' the Medina Yard in mock battles, supervised by umpires. On one memorable occasion, the army was repelled by a shower of fake wooden hand grenades which rained down from the roof of Medina House. As the invaders dodged them, a horde of policemen swarmed out—like Keystone Cops—from the Birmingham Road police station and disarmed all the soldiers. Uffa was delighted to accept their surrender and presented the commanding officer with a brace of pheasants which had been 'accidentally shot from the sky' during the mêlée.

The German's bombing of the Isle of Wight would reach a terrible peak on the night of 4–5 May 1942, known since as the Cowes Blitz. The attack began at around 11 pm with waves of German planes dropping parachute flares and incendiary bombs. A second wave of aircraft arrived at 2:00 am and attacked with high-explosive and armour-piercing bombs. Over 200 tons of explosives were dropped that night, many buildings were destroyed and more than seventy people died. The Luftwaffe, however, did not find Cowes an easy target. A Polish destroyer, ORP *Błyskawica*, had been moored alongside the J S White Shipyard during repairs and alterations. She had originally been built in Cowes and returned several times during the war. Her captain, Commander Wojciech Francki, had defied an order from the British Admiralty to remove her armaments while she was in dock, and had kept good supplies of ammunition on board. He and his crew fought back valiantly. They lit smoke cannisters to obscure the dockyard and brought their heavy calibre guns to bear on the enemy aircraft. This forced the Luftwaffe to fly higher than they had intended, and greatly reduced their accuracy. Her guns grew

The Polish destroyer, ORP *Błyskawica*, was originally built in Cowes and played a heroic role in the town's defence during the 'Cowes Blitz' of 1942.

so hot that the crew drew seawater to cool them, and some suffered burns to their hands. *Błyskawica* was supported by smaller calibre weapons from the six Free French Naval units based in Marvin's Yard further south, and the local ARP anti-aircraft guns.

Commander Francki recorded in his report, 'The ship fired her 40 mm guns and heavy machine guns by sound, which was usually possible when the planes dived before dropping their bombs, or by locating the position of the plane with the help of the searchlights on the island. Fire was always spread both in direction and elevation. The results appeared good to me, as very often the planes turned violently, which we could plainly hear. Once about 24:00 we saw a plane in a very dense stream of machine gun bullets. About 05:00 in a 40 mm shell barrage, we saw a large explosion, much lighter in colour than the exploding shells and from it fell large numbers of sparks. The ship fired 2,030 40 mm shells and 10,500 rounds of machine gun ammunition (13.2mm).'

One of the incendiary bombs had fallen on Medina House but Uffa's Home Guard Unit, supported by firewatchers, managed to douse the flames. Uffa, however, inhaled dirt and grit from the explosion which may have caused the bronchitis which would later plague him. The damage was not as severe as they first had feared, and the building was operational again within a week. The next-door Westbourne House had also been fire-damaged and Uffa was able to buy it and use it as offices.

The bravery of ORP *Błyskawica* and her crew was not forgotten. There are several memorials to her in Cowes and she is commemorated every year by the Friends of the *Błyskawica*, who marked the eightieth anniversary in 2022. The town of Cowes retains strong links with Poland and, unusually for such a small place, there is still a Polish Consulate in St Mary's Road. Today the destroyer ORP *Błyskawica* survives as a museum ship in Gdynia, Poland.

Uffa's first idea for improving air-sea rescue was a folding boat. He had already been given contracts to design protective covering, small sails and paddles for the inflatable life rafts which were carried on all RAF bombers. He knew that Lockheed Hudson aircraft were used for air-sea rescue work, and he believed he could design a folding lifeboat which could be carried in the bomb bay. It would be twenty feet long, made of plywood, and it would be unfolded by the action of parachutes as it fell from the aircraft. From the outset he wanted it to be a complete boat with both engine and sails, giving airmen a realistic chance of getting home. It would also have enough protection from cold and damp to prevent the limb losses and deaths from exposure that were frequently occurring.

Once taken with an idea, Uffa had phenomenal energy

and could get complicated things done at twice the speed that other men would have believed possible. In no time, he and his draughtsmen had designed, and his boatbuilders had constructed, a scale model ready for testing. It was typical of Uffa that no warning was given of the impending test, he simply threw the model off the roof of Medina House, with a few men posted in Birmingham Road to try and catch it, should the parachutes fail to open. Customers leaving the Duke of York, late that evening, were confronted by a frightening apparition: a ghostly boat—suspended beneath white canopies—was slowly descending from the heavens while men in the street waited with open arms. Uffa later joked that some of the drinkers had sworn, on the spot, that they would take the pledge.

The experiment was a success. The parachutes opened and the boat was not damaged. The next morning, having had only four hours sleep, Uffa took his model to London and the offices of the Ministry for Aircraft Production. The minister, John Moore Brabazon, was an unusual politician. He had been the first man to pilot a heavier-than-air flying machine in Britain and received the first British pilot's licence: the Royal Aero Club Aviator's Certificate number 1.[141] Nonetheless, he gave up flying a few months later—at his wife's insistence—when his close friend Charles Royce was killed in an air crash. But Brabazon wasn't grounded for long; he joined the Royal Flying Corps as a pilot on the outbreak of World War I, winning the Military Cross and rising to the rank of Lieutenant Colonel. Between the wars he served twice as a Conservative MP (once for Chatham and once for Wallasey) and remained a friend of Churchill, despite their very different views on Germany. Like many pilots, he was also a passionate sailor who enjoyed experimenting with unusual rigs. He had even attached an engine to a Bembridge Redwing yacht and turned it into the world's first auto-gyro boat. Churchill made

---

141   Moore Brabazon's car bore the registration number FLY 1.

him his Minster of Aircraft Production in 1941, taking over from Lord Beaverbrook, who had resigned, only to come back later in the war as Minister of Supply.[142] Beaverbrook's were big shoes to fill, his management of aircraft manufacturing had been a considerable success and he was credited with increasing production by fifteen per cent.

Uffa knew Brabazon well; they had sailed together over twenty years, and they shared many friends. When Uffa arrived without an appointment, he was firmly told to come back once he had been through all the proper channels. Uffa, however, was nothing if not persistent and breezily told the officials that Brabazon *would* see him, once he knew that it was Uffa Fox who was creating a commotion in the waiting room. To their astonishment, Brabazon did precisely that and immediately welcomed the visitor into his office. Uffa showed Brabazon the model, explained how it worked, and then offered to throw it out of the window as a practical demonstration. 'No need to waste time,' said Brabazon, 'if it worked in Cowes it will work here. You have my blessing. Proceed full speed ahead with the idea. You have a completely free hand, for you may wish to change even the conception of the boat itself.'

Uffa went home to Cowes with precisely what he had hoped for: a free hand, which meant he could work quickly without getting entangled in the petty regulations and procedures which he so despised. His first port of call was to the Fleet Air Arm on Thorney Island to measure a Hudson bomber. He and his men immediately discovered that the size of the jacks controlling the bomb doors did not leave enough room for his folding boat. This would be the first of many setbacks that

142   Moore Brabazon was forced to resign in 1942 for saying he hoped Germany and the Soviet Union would destroy each other. The Russians were then crucial allies and, for Churchill, this was the last straw. Moore Brabazon would later chair the committee which approved designs for post-war civilian aircraft, and he gave his name to the gigantic Bristol Brabazon airliner: a 'white elephant' project which failed to enter commercial service.

he would stumble over, and he returned to Cowes deep in thought. At the Medina Yard it was his old friend and sailing companion, Bob Dickerson, who came up with the solution. 'Can't think why you're buggering about with boats that fold, Uffa. What you want to build is an ordinary lifeboat and carry it under the plane like a torpedo.' Uffa, uncharacteristically, fell silent while absorbing the fact that his folding boat was already obsolete. The next morning, he and Bill Waight were back at Thorney Island, this time to measure the outside dimensions of a Lockheed Hudson.

Remarkably, this wasn't an entirely new problem for Uffa. Prior to the war, Air Commodore Burling, who commanded the RAF's flying boats, had commissioned an 'airborne' sailing boat from Uffa. *Wizard* was an eighteen-foot Jolly Boat designed to travel under the wing of a flying boat as Burling journeyed between RAF Mountbatten in Plymouth, and his home in the Scilly Isles. Additionally, before Uffa started his own boatyard, he had briefly worked for Groves and Gutteridge, who specialised in lifeboat construction. Finally, he knew how to design very fast sailing canoes, and his most successful lifeboats would bear a marked resemblance to them. This experience saved Uffa valuable weeks—if not months—of time.

His second inspection of a Hudson confirmed that it was, indeed, possible to suspend a boat from a single bomb hook and attach it to the fuselage like a torpedo. On returning to Cowes, he went straight back to work to design a new, non-folding, airborne lifeboat. The first draft of his design was completed, incredibly, by midnight on that same day.'[143] His entire team had worked, as he did, from dawn to dusk and beyond to make this possible.

He started from the premise that in order to accommodate an aircrew of up to seven or eight men (sometimes more) the

---

143   Uffa had 'borrowed' some additional draughtsmen from the J S White shipyard for a period of four weeks. A few of them were still working for him four years later.

boat needed to be twenty-three feet long and able to weather a gale at sea. At the same time, it had to offer the minimum resistance to the air while attached to the aircraft without moving the plane's centre of gravity out of its safe tolerance. By a Herculean effort Uffa and his men, working in twenty-four-hour shifts, completed the first Airborne Lifeboat just three weeks later. 'Work went on apace, for I divided good chaps into day and night shifts. The day shift worked from a quarter to eight in the forenoon until eight o'clock in the evening and the night gang came on at a quarter to eight at night and knocked off at eight in the morning. This timing allowed a quarter of an hour at the end of each watch for the two gangs to explain to each other the difficulties they had encountered, and how they thought they should be overcome.'

No sooner had the paint dried, than the first Airborne Lifeboat was on the roof of Uffa's car on its way to Eastleigh Airport near Southampton. It was here that the civilian firm, Cunliffe Owens, received new Lockheed Hudsons, in kit form, from Southampton Docks and assembled them for the RAF, and it was also from here that the Airborne Lifeboat would make its first flight. Once the boat had been installed beneath the aircraft, Uffa met 'Bebs', the test pilot, and asked him what he thought of it.

'Not much,' came the terse reply.

Uffa had anticipated this: 'You fly this machine with the bomb doors open. Your plane is then dragging these ugly shaped doors through the wind, and the wind is buffeting in and out of the bomb bay, and these great jacks that control the doors all out at an angle of forty-five degrees on both sides from the centreline. This airborne boat is much cleaner, sweeter, more streamlined through the air, and much safer.'

Bebs looked thoughtfully at what must—to him and most others—have seemed an improbable thing to attach to an aeroplane. Eventually, he smiled and agreed to fly, with the proviso that Uffa himself accompanied the test flights. Uffa unhesitatingly agreed, and the two men became firm friends.[144] They flew together on many successful test flights, always with a full-scale replica of the Airborne Lifeboat attached to the Hudson. It passed all the tests and Uffa never forgot some of the near-aerobatic manoeuvres that he experienced. 'Up and up we went to a great height, then Bebs cut the engines back and back, until at sixty knots the Hudson stalled and started to drop out of the sky like a leaf, twirling and twisting. After a while Bebs had his machine under control and we flew level once more; then up and up again to an even greater height and this time Bebs put the flaps right down, cut the engines back, back, back and still farther back until finally, at forty-five knots, we stalled and started dropping out of the heavens. Down we went, tumbling, dropping, twisting, and turning with our Hudson completely out of control and falling helplessly towards the earth. This time we fell for twice the time and distance we had before because forty-five knots is a very low stalling speed for an aeroplane, but at last as the fields and trees were rushing towards us, Bebs finally gained control; and we started to level out and fly happily for home.'

Uffa wrote of the last flight, 'We were both in the seventh heaven of delight for this was our final flying trial and like all the others highly successful. Battling with his plane in the last rough, tumbling fall Bebs had been unable to read one of his dials, and it was only with great difficulty that I could read and write down the recordings on mine, so we put an estimated figure in for this missing dial which did not really matter anyway. Next Bebs began to throw his machine all over the sky and did everything except loop-the-loop, all with the Airborne Lifeboat underneath, and when we came over his home just outside Winchester he swooped down low over his house and his wife ran delightedly out in the garden to wave to us, so on we went joyfully to make a safe landing

---

144   It had been a long-standing convention in the RAF that, when an aircraft came out of maintenance, the engineer who signed off the work accompanied the first flight.

on Eastleigh Airport.' The flight trials were complete and successful, but the Airborne Lifeboat still had many hurdles to cross.

In Cowes, day and night shifts continued. Watertight compartments, dagger boards, watertight bulkheads, self-bailing slots, self-righting air chambers and a hundred other items had to be carefully fitted, weighed and tested. The finished boat had to be able to survive being dropped into the ocean, and then fly, sail, motor and be rowed. Neither Uffa nor his men would have much sleep until the boats were completed.

Finally, trials of the actual boat could take place. For this, Uffa and a few of his men were cast adrift in a rubber dinghy in the Solent, exactly as if they were downed airmen. Before long, a Lockheed Hudson appeared over the horizon carrying a real Airborne Lifeboat beneath it. The boat weighed close to a ton and Uffa warned his men that—if the pilot's calculations were perfect, and the boat came directly at them—they should dive over the side to avoid being crushed. The aircraft first flew over them at 600 feet and dropped a smoke flare to help the pilot mark their position and judge the wind. Then he circled, returned, and dropped the boat. All the parachutes opened correctly, and the lifeboat began to descend at a thirty-degree nose-down angle designed to cushion the impact with the sea sufficiently that it would remain intact: '... an explosion blew the parachutes away, two rockets fired out the floating lifelines and we grabbed the nearest of these, pulled ourselves aboard, hauled in the drogue and the other lifelines. Within seconds we had both engines going, the mast up and the sails set, and had a wonderous time cruising round and round in the first full-scale parachuted trial.'

The Airborne Lifeboat was a reality. Uffa would remember this as the most satisfying project he ever worked on, and the one which he was most proud of. 'The Parachuted Airborne Lifeboat [was] possibly the greatest contribution I shall ever make to the happiness of others.' Had it not been for a maverick boatbuilder with unique experience, unique contacts—more than a touch of genius—and the grit to overcome huge technical and practical problems, it would probably never have happened.

One of Uffa Fox's Airborne Lifeboats is dropped from a Vickers Warwick aircraft.

Most Airborne Lifeboats were delivered by Vickers Warwick aircraft (left and opposite above), but the Royal Navy experimented with the Fairey Barracuda (opposite below) and, after the war the RAF used the Avro Shackleton (below).

Chapter Ten
Puckaster

Uffa's mother, Lucy, died suddenly and unexpectedly at the age of seventy-three, the same age at which Uffa himself would die thirty years later. Her unconditional love and support had been crucial in forming Uffa's character, and her loss devastated him. She was irreplaceable and may have been part of the reason why two of his marriages failed and he found it difficult to be faithful to any wife for very long. No woman could ever replace his mother and he became uncharacteristically withdrawn and depressed for several months. Uffa's father, Arthur Fox, was equally affected; he suffered a nervous breakdown following a stray German bomb which exploded close to him when he was walking home, and died not long after his wife. In 1966, Uffa dedicated the first volume of his autobiography, *Joys of Life*, to his parents, and wrote, 'To my father and mother, who brought me into this happy and wonderful world, and from my earliest days taught me to enjoy loveliness and live every moment to the full.'

Uffa had long been a Freemason and was installed as Master of the Medina Lodge in January 1944. To mark the occasion, he presented the Lodge with a new secretary's table—he designed it himself and personally selected the Honduras mahogany for its construction. During the war, many of the Isle of Wight's finest woodworking craftsmen had been assigned to him to construct the Airborne Lifeboats, but Uffa quietly put a couple of them to work on the table. When finished, the table was loaded onto the top of Uffa's car and taken to the Lodge where six stewards were waiting to carry it upstairs and put it into place.[145]

Property fascinated Uffa; he loved architecture almost as much as he loved boats. After sailing, the countryside and music, it was his greatest passion. During the war he and Cherry lived at Medina House during the week and went back to Twenty Acres at the weekend. Cherry, however, had never loved Twenty Acres quite as deeply as Uffa, possibly because it had been built for another wife. Uffa knew the whole of the Isle of Wight like the back of his hand and had long yearned to own the estate at Puckaster—a hamlet near St Catherine's on the southernmost tip of the Island—which included a sheltered cove. Cherry approved and encouraged Uffa to buy it. 'In my lifetime I have visited many homes, gardens and grounds, and Puckaster is the loveliest I have seen so far in this world … I fell deeply in love with Puckaster at first sight … Puckaster Cove is half a mile to the East of St Catherine's Lighthouse. It is the only place on the back of the Isle of Wight where one can land in almost any weather, for here the wind is almost always South-Westerly. The Cove is under the lee of St Catherine's Point and inside the boiling cauldron of St Catherine's Race.'

The owner, a London-based timber merchant, had been trying to sell it for twenty years, but there had been no acceptable offers. Uffa's bank balance, for once, was swollen by the government contracts he had received to build the Airborne Lifeboats, and money always burned a hole in his pocket. With few properties being sold during the war— especially on an island which was regularly being bombed— he fancied he might be able to buy Puckaster for a song.

---

145   The Isle of Wight has the largest number of Freemasons in any British county, other than London, with over 250 individual lodges and approximately 8,500 members meeting in thirty-seven centres.

Uffa's own account of how he acquired the estate may have been embroidered—like many a raconteur, he didn't let the facts get in the way of a good story—but it is too good a tale not to include. In 1943, Eric Marvin, the auctioneer based in Ventnor, had put Uffa in touch with the owner and an appointment was made to visit him at his London home.

'I went into a rapturous description of the property, extolling all its loveliness, even to the little trellised shelter with roses all over it housing the three different wheelbarrows of the three gardeners. At the end of my song of praise, he said quietly,

'"Yes, you can buy it."

'Then he opened the top drawer on the left-hand side of his desk and drew out a piece of paper on which was written,

'The purchase price of Puckaster £ ...

'I wrote him out there and then a cheque for the ten per cent deposit with a hand trembling with emotion, and then drank a glass of sherry and we settled down and had a yarn about things that interest us both.

'Suddenly he said,

'"Do you remember which drawer I drew this piece of paper from?"

'I pointed to the top left-hand drawer, and he said,

'"Now, go down two drawers."

'Which I did, and here was the same legend, but the purchase price had gone up £2,000. His desk had ten drawers in it, and he then asked me to open the tenth drawer, which was the bottom one on the right-hand side, and here again was the purchase price of Puckaster, but now it was £10,000 higher.

'I looked a bit blank and astonished, then he smiled and said, "It is quite simple. People coming to purchase Puckaster can utter ten words of complaint against it and still be permitted to buy it, but each word of complaint costs them £1,000, for I will only sell this property to somebody who will love and cherish it. Even before you have ever lived in it you love it, and unlike the rest of the people who have come to buy Puckaster, you have spoken the truth from your heart whereas they, thinking to reduce the price by finding fault, only increased the price until finally, by uttering more than ten words of complaint, lost all chance of purchasing the property.'"

As usual, Uffa was living beyond his means. Puckaster House was a lot bigger than Twenty Acres and needed more staff—including a butler, housekeeper, maids, three full-time gardeners and a draughtsman. It was much more costly to maintain, but there can be no doubt of his profound love for it. 'Puckaster was the most perfect home one could have, situated in the midst of wild, romantic scenery with its grounds stretching down to one thing on this earth over which man has no control, the sea. Here, on moonlit nights, I loved to have the *Moonlight Sonata* played on the piano and gaze out over the ruffled sea where the silver pathway of the moon glittered and rippled catching every wave top. It was then that one felt free to range the whole world over by just stepping into a boat from the cove. The earth, being three parts water is a wonderful place for those who love the sea as, though to the landsman the sea divides the world, to a seaman it unites it, because once upon its wide waters, he can sail to the uttermost parts of the earth if he wishes to do so. All around Puckaster was the peace and beauty of the countryside, with its soft restful greens, browns, greys, all under the ever-changing sky, always full of beauty.'

Twenty Acres had been sold and Uffa's father, Arthur, moved into Puckaster House. Like Uffa, he loved the estate and the many quiet walks which could be enjoyed, both in the grounds and nearby. Sadly, on one such walk, a stray German bomb exploded close by. Arthur threw himself to the ground and managed to avoid physical injury but was profoundly shocked by the experience. Uffa, and his sister, Ellie, took him back to the East Cowes flat, which they still owned, where Arthur could be examined by his own family doctor. He never recovered and within ten days had died.

There were many outbuildings, including stables, loose boxes and a harness room. Uffa had always kept and loved animals, and before long he was talking to Archie Warren, a well-known Ryde-based stable owner and horse dealer. Uffa had come to riding late in life—he was well into his forties—and many accidents and injuries would follow, including broken arms and collar bones, a fractured jaw, two broken ankles and even a concussion, but they did not deter him in the least. It was not unusual to see Uffa galloping across St Catherine's Down with a broken arm strapped to his ribs.

One day Archie telephoned to offer Uffa a chestnut mare he thought might suit him. At fifteen hands and two inches, Frantic was a 'daisy cutter', which meant she didn't lift her feet far from the ground at any gait—making her easy to ride—and she could jump a five-foot fence. Uffa was five feet and nine inches in his stockinged feet, so she was a good size for him. The distance from Ryde to Puckaster is nearly twenty miles but, although Uffa still had one arm in a sling, it did not stop him from riding her all the way home. Frantic was a former steeplechaser who had been confined in a loose box for several days due to freezing weather and was in high spirits. She took off down a gravel road at a full gallop, with the unbalanced Uffa unable to check or even slow her down. Soon he was passing pedestrians, buses and cars on both sides of the road and was unable to bring her back to a trot until they reached Wootton. 'She pranced, danced, slipped and slid for the next five miles on the icy surface of the road … Different friends passing in their cars slowed down to say gleefully that they were glad to be in a car under those conditions and not on a horse.' He finally brought her to a halt eight miles later in the courtyard of The Bugle Hotel in Newport which, fortuitously, still kept stables for visiting farmers. It was market day, and

Puckaster

Uffa grateful-
ly took his feet
out of the stir-
rups, slid to the
ground, and
m a n a g e d —
with difficul-
ty—to get Fran-
tic into a loose
box before
walking around
the corner to his
favourite pub,
The Wheat-
sheaf. A couple
of hours later,
a refreshed and
more relaxed
Uffa remount-
ed and rode her
to Puckaster,
her new home.

Uffa rides Frantic across St Catherine's
Down.

Frantic would always be his favourite horse, 'Towards the end
of the week I knew full well that I should love her forever.'

It would not be the last time that she took Uffa across the
Island at a full gallop. One afternoon, Colonel Spicer, the
Chief Constable of the Isle of Wight, telephoned Uffa to say,
'We've timed you through a built-up area at thirty-seven
miles an hour on a bright chestnut thoroughbred mare and
are preparing a charge against you for exceeding the thirty
miles an hour limit in a built-up area.'[146]

'I do not believe Frantic travelled more than thirty-three,'
responded Uffa. They both laughed and, a fortnight later, the

146   In 1948, the Isle of Wight Constabulary was absorbed into
the Hampshire Constabulary to become the Hampshire Joint Police
Force. The Island has not, since, had its own Chief Constable.

Chief Constable (who was a friend) telephoned again to say that as there was no legal precedent for charging a man on a horse with speeding, they would 'take the matter no further.'

Whenever Uffa came back to Pucakster, irrespective of the hour or how he was dressed, he always visited Frantic before going to bed. One evening, when Uffa had returned from a formal dinner wearing white tie and tails, he lay down beside her and went to sleep on the straw (he admitted to being 'sloshed'). She woke him later by gently muzzling him. 'I tickled her tummy and went off to bed, and, as I mounted the stairs, the thought entered my head that, although I had often seen Frantic in her bedroom (loose box) she had never visited mine. Therefore, the following day, after we had been out for one of our joyful gallops over the top of the Downs, I rode her indoors. I had often ridden her in through the hall, drawing room, and the library, always having to dodge the chandeliers by bending left or right, but until now had never ridden her upstairs. The stairs of Puckaster are quite wide, easy going, and heavily carpeted, so there was no fear of slipping.' When they reached the bedroom, the floor began to buckle under their combined weight. Uffa avoided disaster by sliding out of the saddle and leading her back down the stairs. It would be the last time she was allowed inside the house.

Uffa kept several of his lifeboats, including experimental types, at Puckaster Cove, and eventually got permission to run his own lifeboat station, staffed by his own men. One evening, having just hauled a boat out of the water following a lengthy demonstration for the Air Ministry, Uffa and Wing Commander Bill Thomas saw an RAF pilot bail out of a Typhoon fighter some five miles out to sea. Despite being tired, they immediately relaunched the lifeboat and set out in the direction of the pilot, whose position they'd carefully marked. Uffa had put Bruce, his black Labrador, in the boathouse, but the dog leapt through a glass window, swam out to the lifeboat and insisted on joining them. The tide was running fast but Uffa made no correction for it, knowing that the pilot would be taken at exactly the same speed and direction as the lifeboat.

A gale was coming up and there was a heavy sea. It was faster to sail than to motor and they were soon at the spot, but the parachute had been seen by several other vessels, as well as a flying boat, all of whom reached the casualty before them, and the pilot was soon rescued and put aboard a nearby ship. On their way back to Puckaster they came across an American landing craft whose three crew were plainly lost. They shouted across to Uffa that they had come from an American ship, and they had been launched to rescue the crew of another landing craft which had been damaged by German bombs off the beaches at Arromanches during the D-Day landings. They had successfully recovered the crew and the damaged landing craft but were unable to rejoin their mother ship in the plunging seas of a worsening storm. Consequently, they were now in danger of foundering themselves. They had been told to head for the Isle of Wight and make landfall wherever they could. Landing craft (unlike landing ships) are designed to travel short distances, i.e., from a mother ship to a beach, and are not ideal for lengthy voyages in severe weather. The crew had no accurate charts and were worried that they might drift into a minefield (there were many around the Island). Uffa left Bill Thomas in charge of his lifeboat and went aboard the landing craft—itself a difficult and dangerous thing to do in the conditions—and guided them safely back to Puckaster Cove.

When all the boats were safely moored, Uffa took the Americans to Puckaster House for baths and a hot meal. They left at noon the following day, having presented Uffa with the only food they had been carrying, seventy-two tins of Gentleman's Relish. They returned three days later to show Uffa the medals they had been awarded for their gallantry and, inevitably, became part of Uffa's worldwide network of firm friends.

Uffa's lifeboats were a success, and the orders kept his boatyard fully occupied throughout the war.[147] He continually developed new models of different sizes, some taking as many as sixteen people. He was a perfectionist who always wanted to improve upon an existing design. One of his many ideas was for an experienced sailor to be dropped within the lifeboat, ensuring that the cold, hungry, seasick and exhausted crew had at least one person onboard who was fresh and knew how to sail. The Air Ministry, wisely, talked him out of this. In one of the experimental drops a dummy placed in the lifeboat was later found to have a hook through its head. Uffa, who had volunteered to be the man dropped within the boat, admitted to the Air Ministry witnesses, 'It would have been my head and my back if you hadn't got more sense than I have. Thanks for saving my life.'

Although the Airborne Lifeboat had originally been designed for the Lockheed Hudson, that aircraft was to be replaced in air-sea rescue work by the Vickers Warwick. The Warwick had been developed as a larger counterpart to Vickers' successful Wellington bomber, but was delayed by a lack of suitable engines. By the time adequate engines were available, the RAF was using larger four-engine bombers, notably the Short Stirling, Handley Page Halifax and—from 1941 onwards—the legendary Avro Lancaster. Warwicks were given to RAF Coastal Command for use both in both air-sea rescue and maritime reconnaissance. By 1943, they had become the principal aircraft equipped to carry Uffa's Airborne Lifeboat.

Nothing pleased Uffa more than hearing from aircrew who had been saved by his lifeboats, and he treasured the

---

147   In 2000, Bill Waight's daughter, Janet Waight, claimed that her father was 'always very dismissive of the efficacy' of the Airborne Lifeboats, and suggested that their success rate was 'no more than fifty-three per cent'. Even this, however, would have been a huge improvement on the twenty per cent success rate of air-sea rescues before the Airborne Lifeboats were used.

letters they wrote to him. Wing Commander Brian Corry, who commanded the Air-Sea Rescue Squadron at Bircham Newton in Norfolk, became a good friend of Uffa's. This unit regularly came to the rescue of American B-17 (Flying Fortress) crews who had come down in the North Sea. On one occasion, Corry answered a distress call from a crew who had ditched near Heligoland, an island very close to the German coast. As this was an especially hazardous rescue, Corry opted to fly there himself in a Vickers Warwick. On their way they spotted another ditched B-17 whose crew of ten were in a life raft. Corry decided to drop his lifeboat close to this crew, whose rescue was certain, and radioed for another aircraft to go to the first location near Heligoland. Both rescues were a complete success. The two lifeboats were each successfully dropped; all twenty of the downed airmen boarded them and sailed back to the east coast of England where they were met by Air-Sea Rescue launches.

Once onboard an Airborne Lifeboat, crews would discover a surprising assortment of useful items in the many watertight compartments. As well as a radio, compass and charts, along with books telling them how to sail and navigate, they would also find fuel for 600 miles, food for a month—including self-heating soups—clothing for ten men, fishing gear, a medicine chest, and even a waterproof pack of cards. When shown one of the lifeboats, Winston Churchill had said, 'It will not take ten men to handle this boat. Why not put a waterproof pack of cards aboard? They weigh nothing and will while away the time for those off watch.'

Airborne Lifeboats were used in more than six hundred rescues. Airmen who owed their lives to them formed the 'Goldfish Club' and Uffa treasured a certificate they gave him which bore their names.

One of Uffa's close friends was Joseph Weston Martyr (1885–1966): a yachtsman, writer and broadcaster, who helped create the Fastnet race, first run in 1925. Many of his stories were published in *Blackwood's Magazine* and broadcast on BBC Radio.[148] Martyr knew Uffa well and his prose portrait of him was published in *Blackwood's* a few years after the war. It so perfectly encapsulates Uffa's strengths, weaknesses and eccentricities, and is written with such humour and affection, that it is worth reproducing here in full. This is Uffa, in late middle-age, at the peak of his powers as a boat designer and *enfant terrible* of the Establishment. Martyr uses the pseudonym 'Odo Hunter' to describe his old friend.

QUIET HOLIDAY WITH A GENIUS
by Weston Martyr
(Reprinted from Blackwood's Magazine)

I live by myself in a little house in the depths of the country, miles away from anywhere. I live a very quiet life and see very few people. I like it.

Odo Hunter lives in a bustling, shipbuilding port on the other side of England, where he is extremely busy, knows everyone, and is never, never quiet. He likes it.

This will explain why I was astonished when, one fine day in the summer of 1944, Odo burst in upon me through the French window of my sitting-room and announced that he had come to stay with me for a week. He added, 'I've got the Missus and a lifeboat outside. What shall I do with 'em?'

As I do not want anyone to think Odo is mad, or was drunk, I had better explain at once that the man is a genius and does not think, behave, look, or talk like an ordinary person. If he did, he would not be a genius. I do not imply that his strange behaviour, queer appearance, and unorthodox manner of expressing himself make him a genius. These things are merely the marks of the breed. What does make him a genius

---

148   *Blackwood's Magazine* was published from 1817 to 1980. Its content was both political and literary, with a mixture of satire, reviews and criticism. At its peak in the nineteenth century, the magazine had a large audience.

is the originality and speed of his thought. If a man paints better pictures, or composes better music than anyone else, we call him a genius. The things Odo creates fulfil their purpose better than the things created by other men to fulfil the same purpose. Odo creates—that is, designs and builds—better boats than anyone else, therefore I call him a genius.

When Odo mentioned the presence, outside, of a wife and a lifeboat I did not rise to his bait. I know my Odo, and I knew the delight he takes in pulling legs. I grinned and said, 'If you really have come to stay with me, I am delighted. But rations for one don't go very far, old fellow, so I hope you've brought some food along.' Whereat Odo rushed to the front door and roared, 'It's all right, Missus. He says he's delighted. I told you so.'

This time I did rise in a hurry. Drawn up in the narrow lane outside my front gate I saw a big car, a small lady sitting placidly inside it, and, behind, a large, blue lifeboat on a trailer.

I stood there, looking like a fool, I expect, with my eyes bulging. Odo jumped into the car and began throwing things out of it into my garden. Among other items I noticed a ham, a crate of bottles, and a salmon. 'Don't you worry about grub,' cried Odo. 'You're as bad as the Missus. When I told her last night we were going to stay with you she wanted me to send you a telegram, but of course I didn't. You might have refused to have us. Then she said you wouldn't have enough grub, and I said what about all that stuff she'd got stowed away in the storeroom, and she said that was for an emergency, and I said this is an emergency. And as I'm a hearty eater we've brought plenty. These lobsters were swimming yesterday. Catch!'

I ignored the lobsters and advanced to greet the lady. She said, 'I ceased to apologise for Odo's behaviour very soon after I married him two years ago. The things he does and drags me into are beyond apologies. This unannounced descent upon you, for instance. He said you wouldn't mind because you and he were old friends. I do hope you are.' I said, 'We've known each other for twenty years and I've learned never to be surprised at anything he does. I'm very glad you've come.'

Mrs Odo gave a sigh of relief. 'Thank heavens for that,' she said. 'I mean ... It's very kind of you to bear with us, but what I'm thanking heaven for is that you really are an old friend. You know, Odo's quite capable of planting me upon an entire stranger, so I've been spending most of the time during the drive here praying you really were an old friend and not merely a chance acquaintance.'

I said, 'Don't worry any more then. I'm very fond of that old madman of yours, and whatever he does is all right as far as I am concerned. He never told me he was married, but I congratulate him now. I don't know about congratulating you, though. I think you are either very brave or extremely rash. But do come in. We'll leave Odo to carry in the baggage. I don't suppose he told you why he suddenly decided to spend a week in this remote part of the world. He won't bother to tell me, either, if I know him. Well, it doesn't really matter; but what I do want to know is, what on earth he's up to with that lifeboat? Has he any good reason for towing a lifeboat by road all across England, or is he just doing it for fun?'

'All I can tell you,' she replied, 'is that when he got home yesterday evening he asked me if I'd ever met you. I said I hadn't, and he said, "Well you soon will. We're going to stay with him for a week and we're starting tomorrow morning, because I'm testing the new boat at Farport."'

Here Odo pranced in upon us. The man seldom walks. He is so full of supercharged energy that his usual mode of progression is at a trot, dancing upon his toes. He said, 'Ha! I told you you'd get on with Jim, Missus. I've dumped all the gear and grub in the hall. Where shall I put the boat?'

I said, 'I won't have it in the garden. Leave the thing in the lane, or run it into the next field.'

'Can't be done,' said Odo firmly. 'That boat's precious. More than rubies. And fragile. Got to be, you understand for lightness. And she's bung-full of priceless gear. The wireless alone ... Why! there's over £300 of navigating instruments in her. Leave her in the road and the boys of the village will tear her to pieces. Put her in the field and the cows will eat her. Besides, she's a Number One, Air Ministry, Priority Secret. Prototype boat. For the Pacific. If the Ministry only knew I'd brought her by road, all this way, stark naked on a trailer … Well, anyhow, I averaged thirty all the way and never stopped once, except for lunch and four or five times for beer, so nobody's had much chance to gaze at her. She'll have to go under lock and key here, though. Haven't you got a garage?'

I said, 'Yes. It's twenty feet long, and your boat's thirty at least. And it hasn't got a lock, anyway.'

'There's no building you can lock her up in this village,' I answered. 'All I can suggest is that you run her back to Chemton—it's only about 16 miles-and see if the police can help you.'

Odo said, 'You're not trying, Jim. Where's all that noise coming from?'

'Airfield, just the other side of those trees,' I answered.

'Well, dash it!' cried Odo. 'Why didn't you tell me that at first? It's exactly what's wanted. Missus, we'll be back in twenty minutes. Make the tea. Jim, jump in the car and pilot me.'

I said, 'It's an American airfield, old chap, and they're very fussy. Won't let anyone near the place. I've tried to have a look at it several times, but they've posted MPs everywhere, all hung about with pistols and tommy-guns. I'm told they shoot to kill, too.'

Odo said, 'Pah! Come on. Get in! Don't be so faint-hearted.'

I got in. We drove off. I said, 'You'll never get into that airfield.'

Odo said, 'I will.' I said, 'How?'

Odo said, 'Somehow.'

'Well, there's the MP,' I said. 'Just ahead, on the corner. And I'm going to switch off your ignition if you try to drive past him.'

UFFA – Yachting's Eccentric Genius

The MP said, 'Halt! Show your pass, mister.' Odo said, 'Sorry. I haven't got a pass.'

The MP said, 'Then you'll have to go back, brother.'

Odo said, 'I can't back with this trailer behind. And I can't turn round in this lane.'

The MP laughed. 'I guess you're right.' he said. 'You'll have to go ahead now. Straight ahead and out by the main gate. Keep going and no monkeying around, mind! I'll phone through and warn 'em you're coming.'

We proceeded. Odo said, 'We're in.' I said, 'Well, I'll be damned.'

Odo said, 'I'll bet that's headquarters, with the Stars and Stripes flying over it. We'll try it, anyway.'

He drew up in front of the building and went in. Presently he came out again, with a major, who shook hands with him and said, 'Well, good-bye, sir. Glad to have met you, Mr Hunter. That boat of yours sure looks bully. Drive her into the hangar and leave her there as long as you like. She'll be quite OK. We keep a sentry on duty in that hangar, day and night.'

We left the lifeboat in the hangar and drove homewards. I said, 'How on earth did you do it?'

Odo said, 'Oh, just told him I wanted him to lock up a lifeboat for me. I think he thought I was drunk; but when he heard it was an Air-Sea Rescue lifeboat I'd designed specially for long distance work in the Pacific, he couldn't do enough for me. He said he guessed I'd save the lives of a whole lot of their boys out there. He guessed right. And here we are, home again, and I told the Missus we'd be back in twenty minutes and we are.'

Mrs Odo had made the tea and set it out in the garden all ready for us. She said, 'I made myself at home in your kitchen. I hope you don't mind.'

I said, 'It's very clever of you to do it, and I don't know how you found where everything was.'

Odo said, 'Yes, the Missus is clever. I've seen her do

miracles.' I said, 'Miracles! Then you're a good pair. I've just been watching him perform miracles, too, Mrs Odo.'

'I know,' she said. 'I mean, Odo never stops talking, as you know. But when he does stop and sits, laughing at himself, like that, then I know he's been up to something clever, or naughty. What have you done now, my pet?'

'Oh, nothing.' answered Odo. 'And I'm not laughing at myself. I'm laughing at Jim. He's just seen me do something quite simple and straight forward, but, because he made up his mind beforehand it was going to be impossible, the old chump thinks I'm wonderful. And don't call her Mrs Odo any more, Jim. It sounds awful. Her name's Jane, but she answers best to Missus. Have some Gentleman's Relish on your toast, old sailor. I got hold of six dozen pots of it on D-Day plus One. Found some Americans drifting about in a broken-down landing barge and towed 'em in, and they gave me the stuff. As a mark of esteem and gratitude, they said, but really because they'd had nothing else to eat for thirty hours and they never wanted to see any more of it as long as they lived. Don't ask me where they got it. The thing that struck me was that after eating nothing else but this stuff, neat, for a day and a half, none of 'em were seasick. Have some more, Missus.' 'I will not,' said she. 'It's rather rich, but you've made it sound much too rich. Instead of talking nonsense, hadn't you better tell Jim precisely why you've dumped yourself, your wife, and your lifeboat upon him without any warning or apology?'

'Perfectly simple,' said Odo. 'I needed a holiday. What's more, I wanted a holiday. I haven't had one since the war began. I wanted a week's peace and quiet. And the boat was ready for testing. Also I was scheming to gain time, because I've another and better boat coming along. So I told the Ministry people I'd be ready to test this boat in a week's time, from Farport. They said, "Why now, and why Farport?" And I said, because I've got to have a week's absolute quiet and rest, and Farport was the nearest port to Jim's garden, which was the quietest, restfullest place I knew. So I proposed going there. So here we are. I'm going to sit here in the sun, and eat and sleep and do nothing for a whole week. I'll do nothing. Nothing at all. Except I've got to deliver the boat to the RAF soon at their airfield near Farport, to let 'em fit her to her carrier aircraft, ready for the test drop. By the way, Jim, you're going to help me with the test drop.'

'Me!' I cried. 'Don't you believe it. I don't know what plan you've got in your horrid mind, but I do know I'm not going to let you drop me in a boat, out of an aircraft, into the cold North Sea. I'm too old for such games.'

'Nonsense,' replied Odo. 'All I want you to do is to let the Navy dump you in a rubber boat about 20 miles offshore. You'll represent a ditched bomber's crew. The rescue aircraft will fly out, and, when and if she finds you, she drops the lifeboat on parachutes and you get aboard and sail back to Farport. Nice little yachting trip for you. You'll enjoy it. Anyhow, you've got to come. I must have a man who can handle and sail a boat, and I'm absolutely relying on you. That's one reason I came here.'

I protested—hard. But, as I thought the thing over, it seemed to me it would be a very interesting operation to see. And Odo was relying on me, and we were old, tried shipmates. So I said I would do it, if I could wangle a day off duty from my chief in the Royal Observer Corps.

Then the Missus said, 'Oh, Odo! What a shame.'

Odo said, 'Nonsense. It's yachting at the Government's expense. I knew he couldn't resist it.'

The Second Day of Odo's quiet and restful holiday began quietly. He announced that he would have his breakfast in bed, just to assure himself that he really was on holiday. He then slept solidly until tea-time. After tea he arose, a genius refreshed, and took the Missus and me to call on the American major at the airfield. The rest of the day was not quiet or restful.

Puckaster

If Americans like you they do not disguise the fact. They took to Odo immediately and completely. They took to the Missus, of course. And they even took to me. They gave us their airfield. They put us on the roof of the Control Tower, and dive-bombed us with a squadron of Mustangs. They took us up in a Flying Fort, just to see what my garden looked like from the air. They gave us quantities of something memorable, called 'Rye and Coke', in large glasses full of crushed ice. They gave us dinner, and I shall not forget the chicken a la Maryland, the corn on the cob, and the ice-cream made of cream. After dinner they sat us in saddle-back chairs in their movie-theatre and showed us Hollywood's very latest colour film. They took us to the Mess and plied us with more crushed ice plus notable flavourings. We did not get home until two o'clock in the morning.

I said, 'Gosh! What a night. I thought you came here for peace and rest, Odo.'

Odo said, 'I did. And I'm getting 'em. I've had sixteen hours' sleep in the last twenty-four, and now I'm going to have seven more. Be realistic, Jim.'

The Third Day of Odo's peaceful holiday commenced at nine a.m. when he arose, cooked breakfast, and brought me mine in bed. It is pleasant to awake to the smell of coffee and bacon. I said, 'This is very kind of you, Odo.'

He said, 'Not at all. I merely wanted to get you in a good temper this morning. I've got to deliver the boat to the RAF today, and you've got to help me. The Missus has struck. She intends to sleep all day under your apple trees. You probably do, too, after last night. But you can't. It's your fault for living in a county that's all narrow lanes with right-angled corners. Towing a 30-foot trailer in these parts is a two-man job.'

We collected the boat from the hangar, eluded, with difficulty and tact, further American hospitalities, and set off on our 30-mile drive to Farport. In our first half-mile, at the bottom of a hill, at a corner, we met a traction-engine, towing a threshing machine and a trailer full of coals. The lane was too narrow to allow us to pass, and neither outfit could go astern. I reviewed the deadlock, and decided at once it was a situation with which only a genius could cope. I sat back and lit my pipe. The driver of the tractor took much the same view as I did of the position. Said he, 'Somebody'll have to build a ruddy by-pass before we gets out of this mess.'

Odo said, 'We could uncouple the trailer and get a horse, if we knew where to get a horse, and tow it back up the hill and into the nearest field-gate. But that's going to take too long. I'll go back to the airfield and get the Yanks to lend us their crash outfit. I won't be long.'

He was not long. Neither were the Americans. I think it speaks well, both for Odo and our gallant Allies, that we were under way again in less than three-quarters of an hour. What is more, this time we proceeded with an American MP on a motorcycle ahead of us, to keep our way clear. We gained the main road without further trouble, and here our escort left us, after presenting me with a packet of cigarettes and Odo with a packet of chewing-gum.

Odo drove on. Presently he said, 'Some people don't, but I like 'em.'

I said, 'What? Those chewing-gum things?'

Odo said, 'No, Americans.' He drove on at thirty knots. In due time we came to the RAF airfield, and drew up in front of the orderly room. A Group Captain appeared. He looked at the boat and he looked at Odo, and he appeared to be perturbed. He said, 'D'you mean to tell me you've brought that boat all across England without any cover on her?'

Odo said, 'No, sir. I didn't mean to tell you, but now you've noticed it. I'll admit I brought her stark naked all the way.'

'Good gracious, man,' the Group Captain exclaimed. 'Don't you know that boat is a Number One Priority Secret?'

Odo said, 'No, she isn't, sir.'

The Group Captain said, 'But I tell you she is. I've had

special instructions to that effect, direct from the Ministry. She's Most Secret, I tell you.'

'Don't you believe it,' said Odo. 'Since she left my yard she's been seen and admired by several hundred people. I left her in a public car park while I ate, and outside four or five pubs while I drank, and every time when I got back to her I found several score of people climbing all over her. So, whatever the Ministry says, I say she isn't secret.'

The GC said, 'You are Mr Hunter, I take it? Ah! They warned me not to be surprised at anything you might do. But I must say I'm surprised at what you have done. Would you mind telling me why you did it?'

'Willingly,' answered Odo. 'But, mind you, this is a secret. The Ministry don't know it yet, but I can tell you that the more the Jerries and the Japs know about this boat the better, because she's the only one of her type I'm going to turn out, and her successors are going to be quite different and much better.'

The GC grinned. 'Ho!' said he. 'That being the case, let's go to the Mess and see if they've got anything to drink there.'

The hospitality of the RAF differs from that of the US Army Air Force. The RAF brand is less various but more persistent. Odo and I did not get back to our beds until 3 a.m.

The Fourth Day really was quiet. It was also restful, for me if not for Odo, because I had an inspiration and introduced him to a bow and some arrows. The potent witchery of archery then took complete possession of him, as I hoped it would. He shot at a target in the garden all day long, and he would have shot all night, too, if the light had not failed him.

On the Fifth Day, Odo's fingers were so sore from the friction of the bow string that he could not draw his bow. He said, 'Oh! What a terrible pity! I've just discovered the most difficult and therefore the most enthralling sport there is and now, hang it! it's maimed me. What shall we do today?'

I said, 'Personally, I've got to get back to work. The Observer

Corps gave me a week's holiday, but today's the end of it. I've got to go on duty now and I won't be back until the evening.'

Odo said, 'Then I'll come with you. I'd like to see what you Observer chaps are up to.'

I said, 'I'm afraid you can't. I work in the Ops Room at the Chemston Centre. You talk about your Air Ministry Priority Secrets, but we really are secret. We keep ourselves locked up, with wardens on guard, and no one can get in or out without our special pass. The Corps doesn't like publicity. In fact, we hate it. Winston himself couldn't get into the Centre without a pass, so I'm afraid you can't either.'

Odo said, 'Ho! Very exclusive, aren't you? Then I'll amuse myself today. And, look here! How about the test drop tomorrow? If you're on duty, you won't be able to come.'

I said I would ask my chief for a day off, and I trusted he would not give me one. I then fled.

At midday I was busy in the Ops. Room, helping to keep track of the hundreds of aircraft which were flying over our area, when I heard the stern voice of the Centre controller speaking through my earphones. It said, 'The commandant wishes to see you in his office immediately. The warden has caught a man breaking into the Centre through the canteen window, and the man says he's a friend of yours.'

I said, 'Oh, Lord! Odo!!'

The controller said, 'As you do appear to know the chap you'd better hurry. The police have already been sent for.'

I found the commandant seated at his desk, looking outraged and very angry. In front of him stood Odo, looking naughty.

The commandant said, 'This person was caught in the act of breaking into the Centre. He has no pass, not even an Identity Card. He says he's a friend of yours.'

I said, 'I'm afraid he is, sir.'

'Then I will be glad,' the commandant said, 'if you can explain what he thinks he's doing, breaking in here like this.

It's a serious business. I've sent for the police to deal with him. And, if you had anything to do with this, I warn you I shall take severe disciplinary action.'

Here Odo horrified me by remarking, 'Jim's responsible for the whole thing, commandant. He told me no one could possibly get in here without a pass, so I thought I'd show him how wrong he is. Also, I wanted to see you to ask you to let Jim take tomorrow off, because, you see, I'm relying on him to help me bring in an Airborne Lifeboat the RAF are dropping for me off Farport. I hope you will let him come, otherwise it will upset all the arrangements.'

The commandant gasped, 'What's this?' he cried. 'I have been warned by the RAF about this lifeboat test. It's most secret. And here you come, breaking in here, and telling me all about it. Who are you?'

'Hunter's the name,' replied Odo. 'It's my lifeboat.'

'Good gracious!' the commandant exclaimed; 'are you Odo Hunter? I heard you were making these boats. Why didn't you say who he was at first, Jim. Very stupid of you. It would have saved all this-er-nonsense. I owned one of your yachts once, Mr Hunter. *The Vixen*, in 1925. I won, or rather she won all the local races that season. She was a real little beauty, and I'm very glad to meet her designer. Now, let's see. Sit down, Mr Hunter, do. And you, Jim, run along. Get back to the job. And tell the warden we shan't need the police after all.'

I did as I was bid and returned to my work in the Ops. Room. Presently I observed Odo entering our Holy of Holies. He was escorted by no less a person than the commandant, who showed him everything. All Odo said to me was, 'Passes, my foot!'

When I got home Odo said, 'You nearly lost your job today, my son.'

I said, 'Yes. Thanks to your nonsense, you old maniac.'

But Odo said, 'No. Thanks to me, you've kept it. Your boss took me out to lunch, and he said he wouldn't give you tomorrow off, so I'd better let him go instead of you. However, I resisted his artfulness, and he's letting you go. Told me to tell you so. Aren't you pleased with me for arranging it so nicely?'

We started for Farport at five o'clock next morning. When we were fifteen miles from anywhere Odo said, 'You'd better take off your coat and tie and hide 'em in the back of the car before we get to Farport. You'll find a dirty old fisherman's pullover in my bag. Put that on.'

I said, 'What for?'

Odo said, 'Because you're my bos'n, and you've got to look like a bos'n. I have to keep on telling you this is Most Secret. If the Navy or the RAF find out you're a mere civilian, butting in on this, they'll probably shoot you.'

I said, 'Hang it, Odo, I don't know that I like this.'

Odo laughed and accelerated. 'You can't back out now,' said he. 'And Farport's a naval base these days. All barbed wire and sentries. I'll get you in all right on my overall pass as my bos'n, but when we are in you'd better begin calling me "Sir" and "Mr Hunter". There'll be all sorts of Ministry VIPs coming out with us in the destroyer, so you'd better act your part properly and no nonsense. Carry my bag when we go aboard, and all that.'

There was no getting out of it now for me. I could not even get out of the car. Odo saw to that. He drove at fifty miles an hour and skidded round all corners. So I said, 'Very good, sir. Mr Hunter, you're a kidnapping, double-crossing, old scoundrel.'

We reached the quay at Farport at 06.10 hours, and found a destroyer, a naval Commander, two Wing Commanders, and several important-looking civilians awaiting us.

The Commander said, 'Good morning, Mr Hunter. You're ten minutes late so we'd better get aboard at once and get cracking.'

Odo said, 'Right, sir. I'm sorry I'm late. Bos'n, where's my bag?'

'I've got it, Mr Hunter,' I said, 'Leave it to me, sir.'

Puckaster

'Hullo!' exclaimed the Commander, staring hard at me. 'What are you doing here?'

I said, 'Oh, lawks!'

Odo slapped his leg and burst out laughing. 'Rumbled!' said he. 'I might have known you can't slip anything past the Navy.'

The Commander said, 'We met at Plymouth, after the last Fastnet Race, if you remember. I'm glad to meet you again, but what are you doing here? I've got to know, I'm afraid.'

'When in trouble, tell the truth.' said Odo. 'I've given my regular bos'n a holiday, Commander. And I asked Jim here to take his place for the job. He's got no official permit, but you know him and I know him. Also, if you don't let him come, this test drop doesn't come off, because I'm not going without Jim. What about it?'

I could see the Commander thinking things over, even though it took him only a tenth of a second to decide. 'Oh, come aboard,' said he. 'It's highly irregular, but I'll take the responsibility. Let's go.'

Highly irregular? Maybe. But God bless the Royal Navy, I say. It does get things done.

I said, 'Thank you, Commander. And from now on, Odo, you can carry your own damned bag.'

Our destroyer fled out of the harbour and proceeded eastwards at the rate of knots.

'The North Sea, or German Ocean,' remarked Odo, looking at the brown water flecked with white wavetops. 'When you and I get aboard our little rubber raft, old shipmate, we're going to get wet.'

'How far out are we going?' I asked.

'About 20 miles,' Odo answered. 'We've got to get out of sight of land, because these Ministry blokes are very jealous and they don't want anyone else to see what's going on. Now, let's go and scrounge some breakfast, for heaven knows when we shall next taste grub.'

At 7.20 our ship went full speed astern and stopped. Two

seamen dropped a rubber raft overboard and held it there while Odo and I climbed in. They handed us two smoke-floats and a camera in a rubber bag. One Wing Commander said, 'Don't make smoke until you identify the rescue aircraft.' The other Wing Commander said, 'Take a photo of the dummy before you touch anything.' And the Commander said, 'Good luck, chaps. Hold Tight! We're off.' At 7.25 the destroyer was steaming full speed away from us, and soon grew small on the horizon.

Odo said, 'Nice work.'

I said, 'What's he rushing off like that for and leaving us here all alone?'

'U-boats,' answered Odo. 'It isn't healthy to keep a ship stopped in these waters very long.'

I said, 'Gosh! I'm beginning to feel lonely. I hadn't thought of U-boats. And what about hostile aircraft?'

'That's why the Wing Commander told us not to make smoke until we were sure,' Odo answered.

'I wish I'd stayed at home,' I said. 'I like this job less and less the more I have to do with it. I'm sitting in the wet and I think I'm going to be seasick. In all my life I've never even felt seasick, but there's something so horrid and leery about the movements of this dreadful raft that I do believe I'm going to spoil my record.'

'Same here,' said Odo through clenched teeth. 'It's not the pitching or the rolling, but the creepy-crawly way the bottom o' this thing heaves and bulges and sinks under you that … '

I said, 'Shut up! Don't talk about it.'

Here Odo dived overboard. Presently he reappeared and hung on to the side of the raft 'That's better,' said he. 'Being in that raft felt like sitting on a lot of soft, undulating blondes. Horrible. In another two seconds I'd have lost my breakfast.'

I clenched my teeth on my breakfast and managed to keep it with me. 'When,' I asked, 'are we due to be rescued?'

'Eight o'clock,' answered Odo. 'What time is it now?'

'7.55—and I hear an aircraft,' I said.

'Chuck a smoke-float overboard then,' said Odo. 'Let's get cracking. I'm getting cold.'

I said, 'Wait a bit. I can see it now to the east of us. A black twin-engined machine, at about a thousand feet. Odo, I don't like the look of him. He may be hostile, coming in from the eastward like this.'

'I thought you told me you Observer Corps chaps could identify any aircraft as soon as you heard it,' Odo remarked.

'So we can,' I said, 'provided we've seen or heard a similar aircraft before. But I've never seen or heard anything like this one. It's coming straight for us and losing height. It's rather like a Wellington, but it's too big. And where's the lifeboat anyway? I can't see it about her anywhere. I think we'd better stand-by to duck.'

'You wouldn't see the lifeboat,' said Odo. 'It's designed to make a snug fit under the Warwick's underbody.'

'Of course!' I cried, for I was much relieved. 'A Warwick. I've not seen one before, but that's what it is.' I set off a smoke-float. The Warwick circled twice and then headed for us at less than a thousand feet, dead up wind. And then a series of miracles happened, or so it seemed to me. The bottom of the aircraft fell off and hurtled down, straight at us. I prepared to dive overboard, but I stayed where I was when three enormous parachutes materialised above the falling object. Three rockets then shot out of the thing trailing bright yellow ropes. 'Sea anchor and two lifelines,' said Odo. 'Isn't it lovely. All going like clockwork. Now watch the self-righting chambers grow on each end of her. It's rubber and compressed air doing that.'

I saw the boat take on, in mid-air, the characteristic shape of a lifeboat with its short lengths of high, cambered deck at bow and stern. Then the boat hit the water within 20 yards of the raft, the parachutes detached themselves, and I became enveloped in acres of clinging silk fabric and several miles of cord. Odo was already aboard the lifeboat when I emerged from my canopy.

'Well done,' said he. 'You've saved two 'chutes. Try and grab the other one. It's just going under water on your starboard beam.'

I said, 'I've got all the parachutes I need.'

Odo said, 'All right. Let it go then. It only cost a couple of hundred pounds; and you're a taxpayer.'

I retrieved the third parachute and paddled my raft alongside the lifeboat. I climbed aboard. Odo was taking photographs of a dummy man who lay strapped on the bottom amidships. I saw a heavy steel hook sticking into the thing's head.

'Makes me feel thoughtful,' said Odo, shaking the dummy heartily by its limp hand. 'I wanted to be dropped in this boat instead of the dummy, but the RAF wouldn't let me. Said they preferred to try it with a dummy first and see what happened. Well, this is what happened. I called them a lot of cissies. Said we were fighting a war, not running a girls' school. But I couldn't shake 'em. Am I glad, now? That parachute release hook dropped 20 feet and weighs 20 pounds. I shall have to apologise to those Wing Commanders.'

Odo began to shiver. 'Burrr!' he said, 'I'm cold. Let's go. In the bottom aft you'll see an armoured-glass porthole. Look through it and tell me if there's anything foul of our propeller.'

'All clear,' I said.

Odo pressed a button and our motor immediately sprang to life. Odo said, 'Lovely. Ship the tiller, Jim, and take her home. We're 20 miles east, true, from Farport. The compass is set into the deck under your feet. Work out the course to steer. There's a deviation table, charts, ruler, pencils, and everything else you want in that locker marked "Navigator". Let me know if the pencils are sharpened. They ought to be. Now, you do the work. I'm going to get myself warm and comfortable. The rum ought to be in the "Medical Stores" locker. It is. And flocks of chemical hot water bottles. Just what the doc. ordered. And here's what I'm looking for. Waterproof, eiderdown sleeping-bag, complete with hood and zip-fastener. I'll zip myself in here with six hot water bottles and the rum, and be as right as rain. Have an Energizing Tablet? No. Well what else have we? Tinned grub and fishing-lines; cans of fresh water and chemical distilling gadget. Barley sugar, malted milk tablets, chocolates, cigarettes, programmes, No. This is the "Instruction Book". "How to sail to windward" in three paragraphs. I wrote most of this book myself, and it's hot. Any ditched aircrew that's lucky enough to get one of these boats dropped to 'em is in clover—if only they'll read the Instruction Book first. Have some more rum. If I wasn't so snug and warm in this bag I'd rig up the wireless and send a telegram to the Missus, saying we'll be home to tea. Can you see the land yet?'

I said, 'No. Only thing in sight is the destroyer, and she's hull down ahead of us, hurrying those Ministry blokes home to lunch, I guess. How much petrol have we got?'

'Six hundred miles of it,' Odo answered. 'Enough to get home from the middle of the North Sea or the Bay, but useless in the Pacific, where you may get ditched a thousand miles from home. That's why I designed this boat to sail. She's got two masts, a jib, mainsail and mizzen, a dagger centre-board plate, and a drop rudder. What she is really is a big, unsinkable, fast racing canoe. Now, there's a nice breeze, and I never did like motor-boating. Let's sail.'

With the help of the Instruction Book (Odo refused to help), I stepped and stayed the masts in no time, dropped the centreboard and rudder, and made sail. Thereafter I enjoyed three hours of real yachting and Odo went to sleep. The boat went faster under sail than with her motor running, and by the time we had reached the entrance to Farport Harbour I had come to the conclusion that any crashed aircrew could, in a similar boat, get themselves safely to land from the middle of the Pacific without much hardship. Indeed, with luck and if anyone aboard knew how to sail a boat, the job of surviving could be turned into a pleasantish yachting cruise.

I woke up Odo and told him so. He said, 'Yes, I know. The

boat's all right, but don't forget—we killed the dummy. And until I can drop a man in an Airborne Lifeboat without killing him, I'll never be satisfied. It's *got* to be done; you know.'

I said, 'All right, so long as you don't try any more of your games and think you're going to drop me. I'm too old and much too scared. Well, there's our destroyer, tied up to the quay. What do we do now?'

'Berth alongside her,' answered Odo. 'And if anyone asks you what you think of this boat, you say she isn't up to her job. Remember the dummy. Also I have good reasons.'

I berthed as directed, and we handed the boat over to the Wing Commanders. They seemed pleased. Said one, 'The flight and drop tests were one hundred per cent perfect. How did your end go?'

'Recovery, motor, sailing, and equipment one hundred per cent,' Odo answered, handing over the camera; 'but when you've had a look at these photos you'll know we'll never drop a man in this type of boat without killing him. The dummy's head was stove in, and the landing shock would break a man's back. And it would have been my head and my back if you hadn't got more sense than I have. Thanks for saving my life. Now I've got to go ahead and devise some completely protective structure and equipment for the man who's dropped and there isn't room for anything like that in this type.'

'Afraid we can't wait for any new design,' said the senior Ministry official. 'These boats are needed in quantity immediately. The war in the Pacific is warming up fast and it's a case of save time, save lives. This boat has now passed all tests, and I'm going to recommend the Ministry to put the type into full production at once. You'll save time and save lives that way,'

Odo answered. 'Give me a month at most, and I'll give you a boat that'll save more lives than this one ever will.'

'This one has passed her tests one hundred per cent and that's good enough for anybody,' said the official. 'The best is the enemy of the good, Mr Hunter, and we can't throw away a whole month. That's quite impossible.'

'Very well, then,' said Odo, 'I'll have to see if I can do the impossible. Good-bye everybody. I'm going home to tea.'

During our drive home I said, 'I don't get the point in your argument with that Ministry chap, Odo. Haven't you and I proved today that the boat is ideal for the job of rescuing a ditched crew, even though a man wasn't dropped in her? I think the chap was right in his decision.'

Odo said, 'If you had a few more brains, Jim, you'd be half-witted. You ought to get a job in the Ministry. It's difficult to make chaps like you see. But I'll try. Listen! What was proved today was that an Airborne Lifeboat can be dropped, on a fine day in a moderate wind and sea, close enough to the target to enable two fit, strong able seamen to get aboard her and sail her home. What was not proved is that the boat can be dropped in a gale of wind and a rough sea close enough to a rubber raft to enable the raft's crew of cold, wet, starved, exhausted airmen to get themselves aboard the lifeboat. The odds are, in such conditions they'd never manage. The lifeboat would blow away from them before they could get near it. As for sailing her home, if they did manage to get aboard, the odds are none of the men would know how to sail a boat, and they'd never get anywhere. That's why we've got to drop a man in the lifeboat who knows all about it. He would clear away the parachute gear, start the motor, pick up the airmen, and show them how to sail home. That's why I want them to give me time to devise something in my new boat that'll keep the man who's dropped in the boat alive. That will save many more lives in the long run than will ever be lost in one month through lack of boats. I know it, but no one else seems to see it. All those lives to be lost just because someone wants to save time. The stupidity of man! It's terrible, terrible.'

After that outburst, Odo was silent for a long time. This is something which never happens to him unless he is asleep—or concentrating on a problem. He was certainly not concentrating on his driving; for the car wandered all across the road, narrowly missed two lorries and a cyclist, and went right-handed round a traffic roundabout.

I said, 'For heaven's sake come out of your trance, Odo, or let me drive.' ·

Then Odo brought the car to a screaming standstill. He smote the steering wheel with his clenched fists and cried out, 'By God! I've got it.'

I said, 'Got what?'

He said, 'I've got the idea. I've got it. But have I got the time? I see how to give a man protection in the new boat so that the drop won't kill him. But it means a change in design. The construction will be a bit tricky. The details want working out, and that'll take time. And I haven't any time. In two or three days at the most I'll get the Ministry's orders to go ahead, full blast, with the production of the type we tested today. And when the Ministry does make a decision like that it's practically impossible to change it. The only thing I can do is to get in ahead of them. I've got to confront them with the new type boat, complete and ready for testing before they make their decision. And that means I've got to get on with it in the very devil of a hurry.'

He then started the car with a jerk and began to drive furiously.

'Not a second to lose,' said he presently. 'Jim, I've got to get back to my drawing office tonight. I'll pick up the Missus and our gear and drive home, non-stop. With luck I'll get to work by midnight. Sorry to leave you like this. But you understand. This job's urgent.'

We drew up at my house to the screaming of brakes and clamorous horn blowings. Odo dashed out, roaring, 'Missus, Missus! Pack up, quick. Now. At once. Got to get home tonight. There's a hell of an urgent job on. Quick, Missus, quick. Hurry. Let's get going.'

Puckaster

The Missus, I must say, reacted most nobly to this unexpected trumpet call to action. She arose from her deck chair under the apple trees without any expostulation or argument and got cracking. She was used to Odo's ways, of course, but still, I had to marvel at her. She did not waste time packing. She brought out a double armful of clothes and gear and dumped them in the back of the car. Odo followed with the suitcases and threw them in on top of everything. He said, 'Good-bye, Jim. Sorry about this, but, anyway, we did have a nice, quiet holiday while it lasted.'

I said, 'Good-bye, Missus. Good-bye, Odo. It's been lovely having you.' I would have said more, but I did not get the chance, because Odo let in his clutch with a bang and departed at speed, blowing his horn and waving his arm out of the window.

I said, 'Well, well, well,' and made myself a nice hot cup of tea.

I needed it.

The house seemed very quiet.

Chapter Eleven
The Flying Fifteen

Uffa was delighted to have Bobbie Sach, his much-loved stepson, safely home at the end of the war. Bobbie, like his mother, adored Puckaster and, for a while, the three of them were very happy. Before long, however, strains began to appear in Uffa's second marriage.

Cherry was not naïve enough to imagine that Uffa had always been faithful—she knew very well he had strayed—but she had, so far, tolerated his dalliances, expecting them to be short lived. Uffa, on the other hand, knew that Cherry *had* been faithful, but that did not prevent him from reacting jealously to anything he considered a lack of loyalty. When Cherry took a brief holiday alone at a hotel belonging to friends, Uffa sent a telegram to the reception desk (knowing it would be read by all) saying, 'If you don't return my wife by the end of the week you can keep her.' Cherry promptly came home.

Uffa, however, as had previously happened with Alma, was becoming increasingly critical of Cherry and the cracks in their marriage soon began to widen. Work on the Airborne Lifeboats had been obsessive and exhausting. There had been lengthy absences from home, endless challenges and long, wearying days and nights of work. It had brought out the best and the worst in Uffa while simultaneously taking a toll on his peace of mind, and Cherry had often been on the receiving end of Uffa's intense mood swings. The end of the war meant the end of lifeboat production and, while Uffa celebrated peace as joyously as anyone else, he knew that the boatbuilding business would be challenging without the well-paid government contracts that had poured into his yard for many years. By October 1945, Uffa had been forced to retrench half of his workforce. He found this especially hard to do—he could fire a man in anger but not so easily in cold blood.

The stress affected Uffa's health. Like his father, he too had been close to an exploding German bomb during the Blitz and had inhaled a lot of grit and dirt, exacerbating the bronchitis which plagued his later years. Passive smoking in pubs—over many decades—probably made it worse. Uffa's niece, June Dixon, believed that his bronchitis may have been a genetic condition inherited from his mother, who suffered from asthma. Today, we know more about the health risks of inhaling sawdust, and a lifetime of working in boatyards may have furthered damaged his lungs.[149] Whatever the cause, it troubled him greatly in his later years and, towards the end of his life, reduced his mobility to the point where he could no longer sail, or even climb stairs.

Orders for new boats were scarce, but the Fairey Aviation Group offered Uffa a contract to design a twelve-foot dinghy which they could manufacture from moulded plywood, then a new material. Uffa was sceptical at first. He had rejected moulded plywood for his Airborne Lifeboats because it couldn't have withstood the impact of being dropped from an aircraft, but it *was* strong enough for a dinghy. Uffa was steeped in the traditional boatbuilding techniques which he loved and understood in every detail, but that did not mean he was blind to the potential of new ideas. The Fairey offer was especially attractive financially

---

149   Carpenters and joiners are four times more likely to get asthma than other UK workers.

Uffa Fox (left) and Charles Curry (centre) launch the first prototype National Firefly dinghy on the River Hamble.

because he would receive a royalty fee on every boat that Fairey Marine built.

He had already designed twelve-foot dinghies for both Oxford and Cambridge Universities, and he adapted these designs for the new material, producing a lighter version which he called the Firefly. It won the approval of the RYA, against stiff competition, and Fairey built two giant autoclave ovens to bake the plywood sections into the necessary shapes. When the RYA Firefly was selected for the British team at the 1948 London Olympics, orders began to pour in, and Fairey were soon building them in the hundreds and, later, thousands. Firefly is still an active and popular class today.

As business looked up, sadly, his marriage took a turn for the worse. Cherry now had firm evidence of his infidelities and she was no longer going to turn a blind eye, nor—as Alma had done—go quietly or cheaply. A bitter divorce battle followed, much of it conducted in public, and it was exacerbated by a paternity suit from another woman, which Uffa strongly denied (Uffa had always said he did not want children and told some friends that he was, anyway, infertile). During the hostilities, Cherry remained at Puckaster and Uffa moved back to Cowes. The divorce was painful, expensive, and drawn out over many months. Uffa's income had fallen sharply following the end of the war and the long battle with Cherry not only depleted his funds, but it also distracted and pained him at a turning point in his career as a boatbuilder. By the time he returned to Puckaster, he was exhausted by it all, but that did not prevent him from entertaining lavishly— always one of his passions.

However—as had happened often in Uffa's unique career—a stroke of genius would come to the rescue. Since the early years of the twentieth century, the American Star Class yachts, originally designed by Francis Sweisguth, had been successful One-Design racing keel boats and had become popular in many countries. There were several in Cowes, and Uffa was intrigued by their keels. They comprised an iron fin with a bulb at the bottom which could be cast as a single piece and bolted to the hull via a flange, and there was also a skeg from the aft end of the keel which extended to the rudder post. At the time, the RYA was looking for a new One-Design keelboat with a 200-foot sail area, that would—they hoped— handle like a dinghy while having the stability and forgiveness of a keelboat. Uffa saw a chance to design a planing keelboat which might be as successful as his planing dinghies, while being affordable to the average sailor.

His first attempt, *Pensive Temptress* (later, the Flying Twenty-Five) was twenty feet at the waterline with a draft of three feet and eight inches, and could be sailed by a crew of two or three. Like the Star Class, she had a cast-iron keel with a bulb at the bottom that was attached to the hull by a flange but, aft of the keel, there was an internally mounted, unskegged, spade-type rudder controlled by a tiller with an extension. The advantage of this design was that the entire surface of the rudder turned, not just the portion aft of the skeg, while it was lighter and created less drag than traditional keel/rudder combinations. Also, both keel and rudder could be removed when transporting the boat. To his great disappointment, Uffa had his design rejected by the RYA in favour of Tom Thorneycroft's National 200 OD class.

Uffa managed to get *Pensive Temptress* to plane so fast that she actually frightened some crews, but she was difficult to sail to windward and the occupants got very wet. He was disappointed and—as usual—immediately set about designing a new and improved boat. When a sailor from Great Yarmouth offered to buy the prototype, Uffa gladly sold it to him (with the usual proviso that he paid in cash) and she won many races on the east coast of England, despite being heavily handicapped.

His thoughts went back to the fourteen-footers which had made his reputation decades earlier. In a long career, Uffa would design and build boats and yachts of every description, but it was his fourteen- and fifteen-foot boats that would secure his reputation as the leading yacht designer of his time and, ultimately, of any time. His old friend, Jimmy Damant, had often encouraged him to: 'Design a boat like the fourteen-footer, but at least eighteen feet long, that will not capsize. Then you would have a sensible, safe boat, that was fun to sail as well, for the rough and tumble of tidal waters like the Solent.'[150] Was it really possible, Uffa now pondered, to design a fourteen-footer that would not capsize? What if you went just one foot longer at the waterline, but twenty feet overall? If, at the same time, you had a draft of only two feet six inches and a 400-pound fin keel, but you stayed with the mast, mainsail, and jib of the International Fourteen, would you not then

---

150   https://flying15.org.uk/flying-15/f15-history

THE PENSIVE TEMPTRESS.
READY FOR SHIPPING, OUTSIDE
OF MEDINA YARD - 1947

have an inexpensive boat that planed but didn't capsize—an obvious boon for older or inexperienced sailors?

Like many of Uffa's best ideas, it came to him in the bath. 'I saw quite clearly the Flying Fifteen marching in triumph before a brisk nor'wester.[151] Her mast, rig, the shape of her hull, the layout of her decks, her shark-like fin keel and her rudder, were as clear in my mind's eye as though the first boat was built and sailing on her trials.'[152] He leapt out, dripping wet, to sketch his vision onto a magazine that had been lying

151   Janet Waight later wrote that her father, Bill Waight, who was Uffa's Chief Draughtsman, also contributed much to the design of the Flying Fifteen, hinting that Uffa took too much of the credit.
152   Fox, Uffa, *Sailing Boats*, Newnes, 1959.

on a chair. He later claimed that he never had 'any desire to alter a single line or detail from my first sketches of the craft'

When the first keel was cast, Bill Waight, Uffa's Chief Draughtsman said, 'That will never work. It's too thin to support the weight of the bulb.' But Uffa insisted that it was strong enough. On the first day of testing the wind was blowing hard. As they came back into the harbour, Uffa said, 'We're going for the slipway', and he went full speed towards it. He had misjudged the distance, however, and they hit it so hard that the shrouds buckled, but the keel didn't move. Decades later, we know that the Flying Fifteen's keel is more than strong enough. As would often happen, Uffa had judged it correctly and proved his critics wrong.

He named the prototype *Dainty Duck*, after his current girlfriend, and set about publicising it in the way that he had always done, by sailing it brilliantly in race after race (usually winning) and writing article after article in every publication

A "FLYING FIFTEEN" FOR THE DUKE OF EDINBURGH: WORK IN PROGRESS ON THE HULL OF THE SMALL RACING YACHT WHICH COWES EXPERTS ARE PRESENTING TO H.R.H. Standing beside the hull are (left) Mr. Uffa Fox, designer and builder of the "Flying Fifteen," and Mr. J. F. Sinclair, Chairman of the Cowes U.D.C. The vessel is to be presented to the Duke of Edinburgh when he goes to Malta. He recently sailed a vessel of this class in the Solent.

he could find. One evening, while listening to two friends playing a duet on the piano, Uffa called out 'Fortissimo!' as the music reached a crescendo. In an instant, he had found both a name and a sail emblem for his new design. Her motif would be *ff*, the musical symbol for fortissimo, and the boat would be called the Flying Fifteen.

In time, it would become the most popular racing keel boat in the world. Today, there are more than 4,000 Flying Fifteens across many countries and the number is growing. They are still being made and, since 1979, there has been a peripatetic annual world championship. Three-quarters of a century after Uffa drew his first sketch, new generations of sailors continue to discover the delights of his planing keel boat. Although some small changes have been made to the hull, Uffa's original design has never really been improved upon.

The Flying Fifteen alone has ensured his legacy will last well into this century, and possibly the next. At the age of fifty, he had repeated the extraordinary success he first experienced in his twenties and, once again, transformed his sport. Put simply, he is the most influential yacht designer in history and his triumphs may never be repeated. Uffa would go on to develop a whole range of 'Flying' yachts of many lengths, all

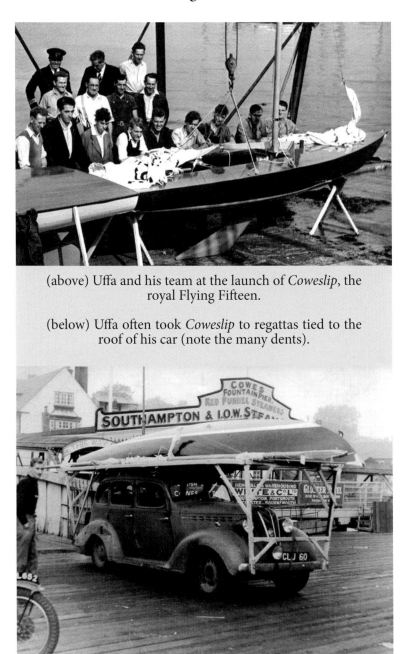

(above) Uffa and his team at the launch of *Coweslip*, the royal Flying Fifteen.

(below) Uffa often took *Coweslip* to regattas tied to the roof of his car (note the many dents).

Uffa Fox and the Duke of Edinburgh racing *Bluebottle*, the royal Dragon, during Cowes Week.

Uffa helps raise the mainsail of a Flying Fifteen.

the way up to fifty feet, with varying degrees of success (there was even a tiny Flying Ten for children). Each one of them had its adherents (many are still being sailed) but the Fifteen would always be the star of the fleet.

Uffa's experience with the Firefly had taught him that he no longer needed to build all of the boats himself. He allowed Flying Fifteens to be constructed by several different yards, as well as his own, taking a royalty for each boat sold. Owning his own boatyard was, now, less important than it once had been.

In 1948, Uffa bought his final property. He was not able

to sell his beloved Puckaster until 1950, but he could no longer afford to maintain the Puckaster estate and its large complement of staff.[153] He wanted, now, to spend more time in Cowes. Another man would have contacted local estate agents and asked them to arrange viewings. Uffa, however, had always liked to live above his work and that meant finding a special building. He had sold the Medina Yard, to his Chief Draughtsman, Bill Waight, along with several partners, retaining only a one-third share and remaining the 'Technical Advisor' of the new regime. That did not last for long; Uffa could never be comfortable as second fiddle in any business, and he soon parted company with the new owners, who, anyway, went bankrupt within two years. It was a sad moment for Uffa when so much of the valuable equipment he had acquired over the years went under the auctioneer's hammer, but he retained the name of the original company, Uffa Fox Ltd. In 2000, Bill Waight's daughter, Janet Waight, recalled that her father 'lost everything', in the failed business venture, and took many different jobs before finding his feet again.

Few things give a clearer insight into Uffa's unique personality and many eccentricities than his letters. They were long, rambling and full of personal insights. In 1951, on hearing of the king's illness, he wrote to the equerry Michael Parker:

> My Dear Michael,
>
> Possibly, because you are so closely connected with the Royal Family you do not realise how the King's illness means so much to us all and how deeply a great many people are touched by this.
>
> Last Thursday, on my way home from a dinner at The Royal

---

153   Puckaster was extensively damaged by a fire in 2014, but there were no casualties. Fire services were hampered by the narrowness of Puckaster Lane and the difficulty of reaching the buildings.

UFFA – Yachting's Eccentric Genius

Thames Yacht Club (where I collected a cup I had won, and had to attend a dinner the night before to do so), my taxi drove by Buckingham Palace and there were all the people anxiously awaiting news. The taxi driver told me how people took their sandwiches for lunch and then spent their lunch hour outside the Palace waiting for news. This letter is to do with the King's illness.

I should be delighted to help in any way, and the only way I know of that I can help is to inform you that Puckaster (the big house) is empty and that it is an ideal place for any man to live after a chest operation.

A doctor friend of mine, years ago, told me that while the London air did no harm to people, it also had no power to do any good—and the air at Puckaster, I can assure you, will make the King eat like a horse and sleep like a dog.

Some three miles away and to leeward is The Royal National Chest Hospital, which is (I believe) the most notable and best of its kind in the country and this is a useful thing. If you have a horse you want a blacksmith's shop nearby and if you have a car you want a garage and if you have a 'chest' it is just as well to have a chest hospital handy, for in it will be nurses and doctors all available for help of any kind.

Within a quarter of a mile is a pub called The Buddle Inn, and the landlord Bill Chandler used to live at Ryde and was an energetic and athletic chap. He collected a 'chest' through overdoing things and Mr Price Thomas, the man who operated on our King, took away one of Bill's lungs in the Brompton Hospital some eight years ago. Bill is now 100% fit and at the moment is away on a motoring holiday somewhere in Great Britain, which is, as you know, an ally of ours!

This sunlit ledge is the perfect place for 'chesty' people, and so I suggest the King comes here.

The entrance is at the north-east end so anyone coming into the hall is well away from any of the rooms (with the exception of the Dining Room) and this is a great advantage, for when we are in our homes we wish to be quiet and private, and defended from people who call by our servants. Also there are times when we wish people to come to dinner and go afterwards and this means they go straight into the Dining Room and straight out—without having a chance to settle down in the rest of the house.

I sold the house in December. I have not asked the new owner about this letter, for as you can well imagine he is sure to be delighted at being able to help the King in any way, as everyone in the land is.

I could take furniture out to furnish the rooms and my Steinway piano, and I am sure the owner would be delighted to put down carpets and hang curtains. I am sending him a copy of this letter and will ask him to ring you to confirm his delight at the prospect of helping the King to recover his former health.

I am also enclosing the following photographs, which I would like you to return:

1. Puckaster from the air.

2. The house from the grounds. The windows immediately above Bruce's tail are the west bedroom and study underneath it.

3. The lawn sloping down to the tennis courts, from the drawing room window, with the sundial on the rock.

4. The King can slide down this bank on air cushions and he will receive £5 if he can break the Puckaster record, which is a quarter way across the tennis court.

4a. Sometimes you only get halfway down before Bruce has you off your air cushion.

4b. You are then out of the competition and have to hold Bruce under the beech tree and let the others get on with it.

5. The King can use a bow and arrow from the veranda outside the Drawing Room window—I will give him half a crown for every rabbit he shoots!

6. When the King is fit enough he can ride over the most lowly downs as quickly or as slowly as he wishes. Just over my head is Jack my old butler. Above him is the bedroom and below the kitchen. The high part of the house was entirely given over to the servants.

7. The rocks and Channel seas in Puckaster Cove.

8. Even if the King does not play croquet, tennis, cricket or have a go at archery, ride a horse, or explore the sea, he will be jolly hungry and look forward to sitting down and eating a jolly good dinner at night, and No. 8 shows the dining table.

The house is empty. It has open fires in all the rooms, but the hall fire will warm the whole house. So please put this proposal to His Majesty the King and let the owner and I know the answer as soon as possible, so that we can prepare the house and then, if he wishes, His Majesty can move in with his servants and staff.

The best train from London for the King would be the 12.30 pm Pullman from Waterloo, first stop Southampton, arriving at 2 pm and giving half an hour to catch the steamer. I can meet him with my 34 hp Packard which is quite comfortable, and he would be over and in Puckaster at 4 pm in time for tea— or of course, he could drive straight down from Buckingham Palace in his own car, or mine, and again catch the 2.30 pm steamer from Southampton.

But before putting this to the King, I think it would be a good scheme to talk it over with Her Highness Princess Elizabeth and the Duke of Edinburgh. I can assure you that if the King gets on this Island, he will live happy and for ever after. Queen Victoria, I am sure, owed a great deal of her health to the fact that the Island is easy to come to from the mainland and Princess Beatrice, our last Governor, lived to be a good age.

Whilst writing I have remembered that the Steinway tuner that comes down every three months from London also goes on to the Royal yacht to tune their piano, and so it might be much pleasanter for the King to have the piano from there over for this, and some more of his personal furniture from the Drawing Room. Then the Drawing Room will become a room of Royal furniture and, of course, would be much more delightful for the whole place if the King had his own furniture. The main thing is that the King should be content and happy and get well.

Best wishes,

Yours ever

Uffa Fox

The new owners of Puckaster were less hospitable, and wrote to Uffa, 'Your proposals are absolutely fantastic and almost amount to farce. We do think it would be better for all of us if you would realise that Puckaster no longer belongs to you and that we are quite capable of deciding who should stay there and how the house should be arranged.'

In the event, Uffa's offer was politely declined by the king whose condition was more serious than the public knew. The stress of the war, along with heavy smoking, had left him terminally ill with lung cancer, arteriosclerosis and Buerger's disease. Within four months of Uffa's letter, at the age of just fifty-six, he died in his sleep at Sandringham, propelling the twenty-five-year-old Elizabeth onto the throne and ending the naval career of Philip.

It was part of Uffa's genius that he could take buildings designed for quite different purposes and inventively turn them to his needs. Just inside the harbour, tucked away behind the greengrocer's and next door to Ratsay and Lapthorn, was an old, dilapidated warehouse with its own quay. It had originally been a public bath—rumoured to have been used by Napoleon III—and was a store for Hewitt's, the grocer's, during two centuries. The mighty J Class yachts had once been provisioned from there, but only Uffa would have seen the potential to make it into a home. He set about turning the upper storey into a spacious house with wonderful views across the Solent, while the ground floor would be his new workshop. His good friend, Jimmy Damant, as well as being Commodore of the Island Sailing Club, was also a local solicitor.[154] Jimmy helped Uffa to put together so many complicated mortgages for the new building that Uffa began to joke it was the 'Commodore's House'. The name stuck and is used to this day.

The early success of the Flying Fifteen was, in no small part, helped by Prince Philip becoming an early convert. The friendship between the two men was, in reality, even closer than most people realised. During Cowes Week, Philip notionally lived aboard *Britannia*, which lay at anchor in the Cowes Roads. Much of the time, however, he stayed with Uffa and the two were inseparable. The quay of the Commodore's House was invisible from the High Street, so Philip could arrive or depart on *Britannia*'s tender without attracting attention. The friendship was based on more than sailing and seamanship. Uffa had the happy ability to get on with anyone, irrespective of their rank or stature.

Shaw wrote: 'It is impossible for an Englishman to open his mouth without making some other Englishman hate or despise him.'[155] Uffa came from the top end of the working class and always retained a broad Isle of Wight accent. Yacht racing, which became popular in the nineteenth century, was considered to be a 'gentleman's sport' and yachtsmen tended to come from the upper middle, or upper class, if not the

---

154   Glanvilles Damant, now based in Newport, is still a prominent Isle of Wight law firm.
155   George Bernard Shaw, *Pygmalion*

aristocracy or even royalty. The yacht clubs of Cowes become progressively grander the further west you go, culminating in the Royal Yacht Squadron, which is housed in a castle, and has been described as the 'world's most exclusive club'.[156] In spite of that, Uffa's charm, humour and international reputation meant that he transcended the usual barriers and was welcomed everywhere.

Philip was, for most of the time, surrounded by members of the royal household who treated him with formality; as well as members of the royal family who treated him with varying degrees of affection (a few openly disliked him), and members of the public who were, in the main, deferential. Princess Elizabeth undoubtedly loved Philip and had done so since first meeting him when they were both teenagers but, once crowned, she did not (as some had expected) delegate any of her powers to him. Although the last queen, Victoria, had entrusted so much to Albert that theirs was almost a joint monarchy, Philip had to content himself with charitable work and plaque unveiling.[157] Had King George VI not died unexpectedly in 1952, at the young age of fifty-six, Philip might have enjoyed a long naval career, but his wife's ascension brought that to an early close. The event marked his 'near-extinction as an individual under the grinding constitutional millstone'.[158] Before marrying Elizabeth, he also had to give up his hereditary title of prince and did not regain it until 1957.[159] He even had to give up his surname, Mountbatten,

---

156   Of the Royal Yacht Squadron's forty-two original members, half were landowning nobility, half were country gentlemen, two were merchants and one a clergyman. Women could not become full members until 2014.
157   During Queen Victoria's many pregnancies Albert stood in for her and became a regent in all but name.
158   Boothroyd, Basil, *Prince Philip: An Informal Biography*. McCall, 1971.
159   Philip was born a prince of the Greek and Danish royal families, but he had to give up those titles when he became a naturalised British subject.

which itself was an anglicisation of the then unacceptably German name of Battenberg.

Only a handful of people treated Philip as they would any other friend, but Uffa was one of them. Another was Commander Michael Parker, Philip's Private Secretary from 1947 to 1951. Parker was an Australian naval officer who did not come from the usual background of royal courtiers. He and Philip had served together during the war when Philip was assigned to HMS *Wessex* in the 27th Destroyer Flotilla of the British Pacific Fleet. Philip joined the destroyer as a sub-lieutenant, the lowest commissioned rank in the Royal Navy. Parker, however, was the ship's First Lieutenant (Number One) and, therefore, both second-in-command and Philip's superior. Despite the difference in military rank, the two men became firm friends. Parker, like Uffa, had a cheerful, straightforward approach to life, called a spade a spade and was unswervingly loyal to Philip. In the Commodore's House, all three men enjoyed each other's company and the relaxed 'unfussy' atmosphere of a boatbuilder's quirky home. Whenever Uffa wanted to contact Philip (or vice versa) they did so via Parker.

Philip's frustration with court life led to him and Parker taking a protracted, four-month, 40,000-mile, world tour on *Britannia*. Before long, rumours were suggesting that it was—in truth—an extended stag party in which Philip's all-male guests caroused in ports across the globe. The Suez Crisis came and went but the tour continued, despite *Britannia* having been, ostensibly, designed as a hospital ship for times of war. On the final leg of the tour, Mike Parker's wife, Eileen, sued him for divorce on the grounds of adultery. In America, newspapers openly speculated that the royal marriage was in trouble. The *Baltimore Sun* went further, printing rumours that Philip was having an affair with an unnamed woman in a London flat belonging to a 'court photographer'. Even the BBC's urbane and measured Alastair Cooke went as far as saying: 'Not since the first rumours of a romance between the former King Edward VIII and the then Mrs Simpson have Americans gobbled up the London dispatches so avidly.'[160]

We now know that the photographer was Baron Nahum, who (along with the actor James Robertson Justice) had founded the notorious Thursday Club and made both Philip and Michael Parker members. Baron (as a photographer he was known by his first name) was a fast-living society portraitist of Italian-Libyan parentage, who had first met Philip on a photoshoot at Broadlands, the Hampshire home of Philip's uncle, Lord Mountbatten. Philip later had him appointed as the official court photographer, but when he wanted Baron to photograph his wedding to Elizabeth, he was overruled by the Queen's mother, who insisted on Cecil Beaton. Baron regularly hosted parties at his Mayfair flat where he introduced bluebloods to 'showgirls', and it was here that he brought Philip into his circle of friends. There are very few photographs of the club's lunches, but one was taken by Baron in November 1947, at a party to toast Philip on his engagement to the future queen.[161] Uffa was frequently a guest of Philip's at Buckingham Palace, and it is possible that he may have accompanied him to Thursday Club events.

Philip did not return to Britain for his ninth wedding anniversary, nor was Christmas spent with his family. As speculation grew, Buckingham Palace issued a statement denying that there was 'a rift between the Queen and the Duke'. Far from dousing the flames, this ill-judged announcement simply poured petrol onto them. When *Britannia* arrived in Gibraltar he and Parker were greeted by hordes of excited journalists. Press interest was now at fever pitch.

In mediaeval times, princes had whipping boys who took punishment on their behalf. The Establishment needed to see a head roll and Philip's whipping boy would be the

---

160   Lloyd, Ian. *The Duke*. The History Press.
161   *Tatler*, 24 May 2021.

The fast-living society photographer Baron Nahum introduced Philip to the notorious Thursday Club.

unfortunate Commander Parker, who was forced to resign. Philip had lost his closest ally, but they remained lifelong friends. His only consolation was that the Queen finally agreed, at Prime Minster Harold Macmillan's suggestion, that Philip be given back the title of prince. In 1982, Eileen Parker wrote a book entitled *Step Aside for Royalty* in which she claimed her husband and the Duke of Edinburgh used the pseudonyms Murgatroyd and Winterbottom to 'gallivant out of the palace'. The controversial 2016–2022 Netflix television series, *The Crown*, suggested that Philip (who knew Stephen Ward) might have attended orgies at Cliveden, the home of Lord Astor.

Small wonder that Philip found solace and escape not only in Uffa's company but in the privacy of the Commodore's House, where there were no courtiers and no royal protocol. Additionally, as much as Philip liked Uffa's relaxed hospitality with its hearty meals, ribald jokes, drinking, singing, and high jinks, so Uffa enjoyed being entertained aboard the royal yacht *Britannia*. At the end of a day's racing, *Coweslip*, the royal Flying Fifteen, would be taken abord *Britannia* while the duke and Uffa took hot baths and changed for dinner. At the Commodore's House, Uffa, or one of his friends, played the piano, but aboard *Britannia*, an entire orchestra played during dinner and a printed programme of music was placed before each guest. Music was Uffa's second love, and he asked Philip, 'What happens if someone at this table wishes to hear a piece of music not on the programme?'

'People who dine on board *Britannia* never ever think of asking for music not on the programme, and as far as I know it has never happened … Write the music you would like to hear on the back of your card, and I will have it sent to the orchestra.' Uffa requested the *Meditation* from Massanet's *Thaïs*, and the final movement of the *Water Music* by Handel. The *Meditation* is a six-minute-long violin solo, and it was a challenging request but, to Uffa's delight, the concertmaster played it immediately and beautifully. Later that evening a musician apologetically whispered in Uffa's ear that they had no copies of Handel's *Water Music* aboard, so they would play the *Meditation* again.[162]

The presence of Philip, throughout Cowes Week, glamourised what had always been the world's most prestigious regatta. With *Britannia* anchored in the Cowes Roads and a Royal Navy warship nearby, a myriad of cameras would always be focussed on the competitors. Anyone who hadn't previously known his name or face, would soon come to recognise the stocky, ever-smiling Uffa Fox, trimming Philip's sails and murmuring advice to him. Whether in *Coweslip* or *Bluebottle*, they usually won and were rarely out of the first three. Uffa was used to being famous, but now he was a celebrity. A local saying sprang up: 'If it was Queen Victoria who put Cowes on the map, it was Uffa Fox who kept it there'.

From 1970 to 1974, another prominent sailor to be seen at Cowes Week was the prime minister, Edward Heath. He too became a friend of Uffa's, but not such a close one as Philip. Heath could be notoriously taciturn, if not aloof, in company. He did not mix socially with those who crewed for him on his yacht, *Morning Cloud*, and they weren't always flattering about his ability as a helmsman. 'He was good at sailing in a straight line,' said one. Uffa was politer, 'Philip is better at the game because he has been at it longer.' Uffa was opposed to Britain joining the EU (then known as the Common Market) and wrote to Heath on the subject. He received a terse one-line reply, 'On this matter we must agree to differ.'

Uffa always reacted angrily to any suggestion that he had 'taught' Philip to sail. Philip was an accomplished and

---

162   In 1958, the Australian-born composer, Hubert Clifford, wrote the *Cowes Suite*. One movement, *The Buccaneer*, was inspired by Uffa Fox, and another, *Royal Visitor*, describes Prince Philip's arrival in Cowes aboard *Britannia*. Uffa made a speech during the first performance at the Royal Festival Hall.

successful yachtsman before he met Uffa, and an especially good helm. Uffa recalled, 'The most remarkable thing, however, was his ability to take a boat across the tide with a free wind. Nine people out of ten fail entirely to make the right allowance for the tide, and when the spinnaker is set this makes the work of the crew difficult. First of all they sail too high on the wind for the next mark, then beat too far away and get worried and start sailing too high again. This means that they are continually altering course, so that the crew are always altering the trim of the sails. This is especially difficult with a spinnaker set, because this sail is set on three corners only by its halyard, tack and sheet. As it must balloon out as much as possible to give the maximum driving power ahead, so the least alteration in course causes the luff to soften, fall in, and shake so that the spinnaker is trying to turn itself round every bit of rigging … Prince Philip watched the land over the buoy ahead, and the buoy astern, and steered so that it did not grow to port or starboard … I have always been greatly impressed by the ability of Prince Philip on all points of sailing, under all weather conditions.'

Chapter Twelve
The Loveliest Music on Earth

W hile sailing in Cornwall, in the early 1950s, Uffa noted, 'Down in Cornwall they describe people round the fifties as getting a bit thick aft. Being past fifty, I was a long way round the equator and this makes it difficult to move around in a twelve-foot dinghy … I realised that what I needed was a more sedate boat, and while racing in all this wind I decided on the eighteen-foot Jolly Boat. It was a boat with all the fun and excitement of a Firefly, but half as long again.' The Jolly Boat was an incredibly fast eighteen-foot planing dinghy that could carry four along with a picnic hamper. It was an immediate success. Fairey Marine built them in large numbers and, like many other of Uffa's designs, they are still raced today.

In 1954 Uffa's reputation grew further with the success of the Albacore, a 'first boat' for those learning to sail that can be raced competitively by those with more experience. The Albacore is a fifteen-foot two-person planing dinghy developed by Clive Dollery and Dave Lowe but based upon Uffa's 1940s Swordfish design. More than 8,000 were built and it remains a very popular dinghy to this day, not only in Britain but across the world. Fairey Marine would, in time, enter the cruising market by producing nearly three hundred Atalanta Class sailing yachts. The Atalanta was a larger sailing cruiser (26–31 feet) conceived by Alan

Vines, a senior executive at Fairey, with Uffa as the design consultant.

In the summer of 1953, Yvonne Bernard left Paris for the coast—as many Parisians do during the heat of August. She spent that month in La Baule-Escoublac, the fashionable Loire-Atlantique resort whose yacht club hosts an annual regatta. Yvonne travelled to La Baule every summer to open her waterside home where she could entertain her friends and guests. As a prominent member of the *Haut monde*, she would be invited to many functions, and at one dinner, the guest of honour was the world-famous British yacht designer, Uffa Fox. He was immediately enchanted by her and she by him, despite neither speaking a word of the other's language.

Three years later, they met again in Paris. They were both in their late fifties, both short and rotund, but had little else in common. There were sceptics among Uffa's circle who

Yvonne Fox (née Bernard), Max Aitken and Uffa Fox.

suggested, out of earshot, that he was attracted to the fortune bequeathed by her late husband, and she was attracted to his royal connections. Less cynical friends, however, knew that Uffa was an impulsive, passionate man who fell deeply in love without hesitation, and they conceded that the elegant widow may have struck a genuine chord within him. Whatever the truth, Uffa lost no time in proposing to her and, as Yvonne could not understand his proposal, he had no choice but to go down on one knee.

Uffa wrote to Philip, 'For some eleven years I have been sad and lonely inside me, but this has all changed now and it is impossible for me to express the joy I feel at the prospects ahead. I have written to Yvonne once or twice every day and telephoned her every day, because her speaking voice to me is the loveliest music on earth. On Friday and Saturday night I had a quiet dinner at the Royal Corinthian Yacht Club, and although I enjoyed the dinner I disliked being away from my home, even though it was only 200 yards, because at home, with the telephone, I feel linked and connected with Yvonne in Paris. If an angel had come to tell me that this wonderful thing of Yvonne and I being so much in love with each other was going to have happened I would not have believed it, and I cannot tell you how happy I am about it all, although, at the same time, I also feel rather humble and frightened.'

Yvonne arrived on the Island in time for Cowes Week, as did Prince Philip. Not even Yvonne could divert Uffa from the regatta, but no sooner was it over than the couple were quietly married at Newport Register Office, and they honeymooned in La Baule. They decided to spend winters in Paris and summers in Cowes. Uffa would pay for everything in Cowes and Yvonne in Paris but, as she soon discovered, Uffa had a habit of spending considerably more than she did. Uffa was, by now, concentrating on writing books and spending less time designing and building boats, so the sojourns in Yvonne's comfortable Paris flat suited him.

Uffa Fox on the roof of the Commodore's House.
1959 portrait by Eileen Ramsey.

Financial problems, however, continued to plague Uffa. While Yvonne was, indeed, a wealthy woman, her inheritance was largely tied up in property and most of the properties were held in trust funds, meaning that little could be diverted to Uffa. At the Commodore's House, the situation was now so desperate that the telephone was cut off, forcing Uffa to take calls at the next-door grocer's shop. During Cowes Week, a two-way radio was installed so that Philip could communicate with *Britannia*. Yvonne didn't enjoy stays in Cowes as much as Uffa enjoyed his stays in Paris, especially when she could no longer use the telephone. The couple never separated, and remained married until Uffa's death in 1972 but, as the years went by, Yvonne's visits to the Commodore's House dwindled to Cowes Week and one or two social high spots.

In 1959, the well-known yachting photographer, Eileen Ramsay, was commissioned to take a portrait of Uffa. She photographed him on the roof terrace of the Commodore's House, in his oilskins, and the picture has since become a classic. It was used on the cover of Uffa's book, *Sailing Boats*, and widely reproduced elsewhere. Uffa leans on the balcony and his face is half-turned towards the camera, with a broad smile, while behind him is the Solent and the estuary of the Medina River. 'He was terrible,' she later said. 'I don't remember how many bedrooms there are in that house, but he tried to push me into each one of them. In the end, I had to tell him very firmly, "I am here to take a portrait photograph of you, and I think we should get on with it!" He and Max Aitken, who lived close by, were notorious friends, and between them, got up to all sorts of mischief.'

Max Aitken (1910–1985) was the son of the newspaper baron and wartime minister, Lord Beaverbrook. An RAF pilot before and during the war, Aitken had fought in the Battle of Britain with the legendary 601, (County of London) Squadron.[163] He became its commanding officer in June 1940 (at the height of the battle) and won both the DFC and DSO. By the end of the war, he had reached the rank of group captain and achieved 16½ kills (one was a shared aircraft). After the war he returned to sailing, which he loved, and took up power boat racing, becoming co-founder of the Cowes Torquay Offshore Powerboat Race. In 1947, he bought the old Ratsey and Lapthorn sail loft at 83 Cowes High Street and converted it into his home. It was just a few yards away from the Commodore's House at 74 High Street, and Uffa

---

163   No. 601 Squadron, sometimes known as the 'Millionaires' Squadron', was established at RAF Northolt in 1925, after a group of amateur pilots had met at White's Club and formed a Reserve Squadron of the RAF. Their battle honours are too long to list here.

Uffa at the Earls Court Boat Show.

was a close friend. Prior to Uffa's marriage to Yvonne, he and Max gained a well-deserved reputation for shenanigans. Like Uffa, Max was married three times, the last time to Violet de Trafford, who was known as 'The first lady of powerboat racing'. When she died, aged ninety-four, her granddaughter, Lucci, summed her up with, 'My Gran was a badass. RIP.'

In 1954 Max Aitken was the driving force behind the 'Exhibition of Ship and Boatbuilding' held at Olympia. It was a success and, with the support of the *Daily Express*, became the annual Boat Show, moving to Earls Court and running until 2018.[164] Uffa loved the event and quickly became one of

---

164   Since 2018, the Southampton Boat Show has been the premier British boat exhibition. Some commentators have linked the demise of the London Boat Show to the move away from Earls Court and the very popular pool area which—although indoors—displayed boats floating in real water.

Girls who had owned or crewed on Firefly dinghies appeared at the 1970 London Boat Show.

its stars, appearing and talking for all of the ten days, always on hand for a photograph, autograph or a pithy comment, and exhausting himself at a time when his health was beginning to fail.

Uffa had always relied on secretaries to take care of his dictation and other paperwork but, from now on, they needed to be able to speak French, as Yvonne could still speak no English and always needed a translator. Claire Gregory was one of several who translated for Yvonne and once did so aboard *Britannia* for a dinner. 'Uffa said, "You'd better be there with her so you can tell her when she needs to go." Uffa was very superstitious and once sent me out at the last minute to find a fourteenth guest for a dinner party; he'd never sit down with thirteen. Prince Philip was great fun to be with. He was always telling us naughty stories.'

Cindy Betley recalls, 'Working for Uffa was fun. You never got paid, but it was still fun. I was a secretary-cum-dogsbody. It was long hours, but I didn't mind. I was his last secretary and worked for him until the last three months of his life. He was in poor health by then. I used to go up to his bedroom every morning with the letters, and every morning he'd say, "If I was a bit younger, girl, you wouldn't be sitting at that end of the bed," and I'd say, "If you were a bit younger, I wouldn't be up here!" It was a joke between us every morning. You never knew who you were going to meet at the Commodore's House. I once had to chase up the road to find Princess Anne and let her in. Another time he was expecting Edward Heath. I went upstairs and told him that the Prime Minster had arrived and was waiting downstairs. Uffa was watching *Tom and Jerry* on television, which he loved, and he said, "You go and tell him, girl, that I've got to watch *Tom and Jerry*, but I'll be down in a minute. Give him a gin and tonic." I went down and tried to have a conversation with Ted, but it was hard work. I'd say, "Did you have a good day's sailing?" Or, "there's Uffa's piano, have you heard him play?" but the only reply I ever got was "Hmmm."

'When Prince Philip was there, having dinner with Uffa, you'd hear roars of laughter coming from the dining room and you noticed that Uffa's Isle of Wight accent got thicker when he was in company. His sister and I would look at each other and say, "It's going well". People say he was selfish, but he wasn't. I was taken ill there once, and he couldn't have been kinder. He didn't always pay his bills on time, but he was a generous person. He dictated a lot, and he was then writing his last book. He rarely got angry, even if you made a mistake. Once, I remember, he came downstairs holding a typescript I'd done from his dictation, "What's this, girl?" he asked, pointing to a phrase. I said "four and a half", at which he roared with laughter and said, "you mean fore and aft!"

'I got the job because I could speak French and I could translate for Yvonne. I always knew if they'd had an argument because Uffa would say to me, "Tell Yvonne to pass the salt". It was less fun when she was there, Uffa seemed to be uptight in her company. One day, Uffa and I had lunch together, just the two of us, and he was telling me about things that he'd done. He knew that I was horse mad, and he said, "I want to tell you something not many people know. I was once engaged to Pat Smythe."[165]

'Every time I left, in the evening, he'd come downstairs—he always came to say goodbye—and he'd say, "Right girl. Now, don't get poked up the pinny, keep sixpence between your knees, and don't forget to go to the loo, because you don't want to have a full bladder if you have an accident." Going to the loo was one of Uffa's obsessions, along with aluminium saucepans, which he believed were poisonous. He was so insistent that guests often went upstairs and pretended to go to the loo, just to keep him happy.

Others confirm Uffa's generosity. Graham Caulfield remembers, 'It was during Cowes Week. At that time it was both dinghies and keel boats. On Friday, we had the prize

---

165   Pat Smythe (1928–1996) was a British showjumper who competed in the 1956 and 1960 Olympics, winning a bronze medal in Stockholm. She was also a prolific author, especially of children's books. Smythe was thirty years younger than Uffa Fox and certainly knew him, but the author could find no record of an engagement. She married Sam Koechlin, a Swiss equestrian, lawyer, and businessman in 1963 and remained married to him until his death in 1985. They had two daughters.

Uffa painting the Airborne Lifeboat on the roof of the Commodore's House.

giving and somebody said, would I take another chap over to the Island from Hill Head. So I did that, on a Cherub, only wearing a wet suit. It was bad weather, and we got very wet. After a few beers, Claire Gregory and I decided to go to the camp site in East Cowes, where we were staying that night. That was when we realized we didn't have any money so we couldn't get over on the Floating Bridge. Claire said, "Oh, Uffa will lend us some." I was a bit nervous—you never knew who you might meet at Uffa's—but we knocked on the door of the Commodore's House to find him at the piano, surrounded by lots of elegant people in evening dress. I remember that the ladies were all dripping in jewellery, and I was dripping water on to Uffa's floor. We stood by the piano while Uffa finished the piece he was playing. Then he cheerfully lent us ten bob, and we went on our way.'

Rosemary Joy worked for Uffa in 1957, having first met him

at his wedding reception. 'My father worked for the Midland Bank in Cowes and dealt with Uffa on a daily basis. My father sailed, and he got on well with Uffa, but the bank manager didn't sail and didn't get on with Uffa at all. My parents were invited to the wedding reception and I was working as an au pair at the time, in Paris, but I was home on holiday, and I went along. My French was fluent by then, and I was later asked to work for Uffa and translate for Yvonne. It was Uffa's first season in the Commodore's House as a married man, and my job was to try and make Yvonne's life easier. I met so many remarkable people. The first was Richard Dimbleby, who was making a television programme called *At Home with Uffa Fox;* there were television cameras everywhere. I also met Douglas Bader, who was a charismatic character, rather like Uffa. There was a nice guy called John Forsham, who we would send out dressed up and with his hat pulled down over his nose. When he walked down Cowes High Street, everyone thought it was Philip and he was able to draw the photographers away from the real prince, who could then go the other way. 1957 was the first year that King Charles was there, and he was then eight years old. When he arrived, I was sent out to buy some soft drink—soft drink didn't feature in Uffa's Kitchen very much—and some steak. When I got to Brawn's shop in the High Street there was a queue, so I asked Mr Brawn if he wouldn't mind serving me first. "You know who it's for, don't you?" "Yes," he said, "Of course I know who it's for." And he sold me the ingredients for Philip's lunch.

'Uffa had a set of little brass cannon. That summer it was quite wet during Cowes Week, and to try and keep Charles amused, Philip's equerry, Michael Parker, fired pencils from the cannon. They did it by opening shotgun cartridges and putting a little powder in the breach and setting it off. And, of course, the pencils shot out and Uffa had got plate-glass windows, and he was very worried they were going to get broken. Parker was a wonderful guy, full of life, and very

Uffa Fox in the drawing office of his last home, the Commodore's House. Image Douglas Glass.

wrongfully treated by the press, I think. I suppose I can't blame his wife. If you're equerry to Prince Philip, you don't get to spend much time at home. Before Uffa was married, Philip spent a lot of time at the Commodore's House but, after Uffa was married, it was a different establishment and it had to be much more formal—because Yvonne wanted it that way—although Uffa didn't particularly care, and certainly Philip didn't care. But there was still a formal dinner for Philip, and I would be cooking and waitressing at those. You didn't just do one thing for Uffa; I typed parts of his books, poured the gin and tonics, went shopping, cooked meals. Everybody did everything. One Sunday morning I was at home when the phone went and it was Uffa, "What are you doing, girl?"

'I said, "nothing at the moment."

"'Well, come to lunch."

"'Oh, I can't come right now."

"'You'd *better* come now. You're cooking it." I went straight there and cooked lunch, it was roast beef. The guests were Air Marshal Sir John Slessor[166] and his wife, and Group Captain Douglas Bader[167] and his wife. If there was one personality that was stronger than Uffa's personality, it was Bader. They were like two exploding bombs in each other's company. They weren't rude to each other but, my goodness, you could feel the power of their personalities. Bader was just magnetic. Uffa's floors were not very even, and they were covered in thick carpets, so Bader had to walk with care, but he wouldn't

---

166   John Slessor held several operational commands in the Second World War. As Air Officer Commanding Coastal Command in 1943 and 1944, he was credited with doing much to turn the tide of the Battle of the Atlantic through his use of long-range bombers against German U-boats. He later became Chief of the Air Staff.

167   Douglas Bader was a World War II and Battle of Britain pilot who overcame the loss of both legs in a pre-war flying accident to become one of Britain's most famous flying aces. He was credited with 22 aerial victories, four shared victories, six probables, one shared probable and 11 enemy aircraft damaged.

Uffa at the Commodore's House with *Kingfisher*,
a Flying Twenty-Five. Image Peter R Keen.

allow anyone to help him, he always did everything himself.
Mrs Bader was lovely; she and I did the washing up. But that
was the sort of household it was.'

Rodney Barton recalls, 'My father, George Barton, was the
Harbour Master in Uffa's day. At the beginning of the war my
father had an office in Shepard's Wharf, but he was bombed
out. So he shared an office with Uffa in the old Medina Yard.
I was brought up with Uffa; he was almost an uncle. I started
sailing with him in Flying Fifteens. I was then just fifteen and
went on until I was twenty-two and went into the army. He
had quite an influence on me and opened many, many doors
for me. The first time I went across the Channel with Uffa, I
was only seventeen and my mother was terribly worried. Not
because she had any doubts about his sailing; what she feared
was what he might do to my morals! She had every right to
be, as well.

'Somebody had their Flying Fifteen T-boned in a collision, and Uffa arranged for me to buy it for £10. It had a damned great hole in the side, but we rebuilt it down at what is now Cowes Corinthian Yacht Club, in the shed there. I rebuilt it with spare bits and old sails. J S Wight's made every fitting for me, but they came out through the back door, so it didn't cost me anything. They even cast the keel. You could relax with Uffa. I learnt so much from him, he was my university of life. One minute you were talking to Prince Philip, and the next to the man who swept the yard. It stood me in good stead for the rest of my life.'

As a seventeen-year-old, Andy Cassell worked for Uffa in his drawing office.[168] 'Uffa was up to all sorts of things. I was a dinghy sailor at the time. One of the things that he got me to do was to sail in one of his designs, which was an Albacore, which I eventually won the national championships with, and to sail out on a reach, then repeatedly fall out of the boat to demonstrate these life jackets which he was trying to sell on behalf of the manufacturer. After a few times I eventually said, "Are you going to pay me any money for doing this: falling backwards into the sea and taking these films?" And they said, "No, we can't do that really, we can't afford it." And I said, "Well, in that case, I'm off."'

In 1963, Uffa was featured on the popular television programme, *This Is Your Life*. It was confirmation of his status as a household name. Yvonne was secretly flown over from Paris and many of his friends, including Peter Scott, Bill Waight, Spike Crews and others paid tribute to him. Uffa was somewhat underwhelmed and clearly did not enjoy a few of the reminiscences. 'You just sit there like a stuffed turd while everyone comes on and says nice things about you. Then, when it's all over, they hand you a cheque for £100.'

---

168   Andrew 'Andy' Cassell is a British paralympic sailor who won gold at the 1996 Summer Paralympics. He founded the Andrew Cassell Foundation, which has introduced thousands of disabled people to sailing.

(left to right) Eamonn Andrews, Uffa Fox and Sir Peter Scott on *This Is Your Life* in 1963. Image BBC.

In 1955, he had been appointed 'Royal Designer for Industry' (RDI) by the Royal Society of Arts. Towards the end of his life, he would be made a Commander of the British Empire (CBE) by the queen but, unlike other prominent yachtsmen of the era, he was never given a knighthood. Perhaps his close friendship with both Philip and Michael Parker, at a difficult time in Philip's life, cost him that honour.

1963 was also the year in which Uffa's health began to decline. Josephine Terry would nurse him for a month before he was fully back on his feet. In 1966, following the International Boat Show in London, Uffa was taken seriously ill. He was now sixty-eight years old and suffering from severe bronchitis with complications. He was, once again, cared for at the Worcestershire home of his old friends, Norman and Josephine Terry. The room they gave him had a bay window with a fine view. One night, while running a high temperature,

A Flying Fifteen is brought onto the quay of the Commodore's House.

he had a dream, 'I was confined to the East Room. During this night this great bay window switched round to the east side of the house in front of my bed, leaving a great space between my bed and it, for as the window arrived, my bedroom floor between disappeared. Immediately this window changed into a great cathedral window with lovely deep Gothic arches, and wonderful stained-glass windows. Now I could hear wondrous, powerful, inspiring, yet soothing organ music. Suddenly, in white flowing garments, friends from out of my past life started to float down from the top of this high window. They swept close to me as I lay in bed, and sank down from where the floor should have been and out through the bottom of the window on a floor lower down … There were both my grandparents, Fox and Cobbald, my father and my mother, chaps I had sailed across the Atlantic with, Charlie Yates from Arreton Manor, departed friends from America, all over England, Scotland, Ireland and Wales, France and Germany, Holland, Norway, Sweden and New Zealand—in fact, from

Uffa batting during a cricket match on the Bramble Bank.

all over the world, all of them saying the same thing, "The sooner you come and join us, the happier we shall be." With my strength at such a low ebb, I was in the right mood and would gladly have joined them. The dream ended and the next morning I was taken off on a stretcher in an ambulance and X-rayed.' Uffa had an unshakeable belief in the afterlife, which helped him come to terms with his own mortality and brought peace to his final years.

In 1967, Uffa, as usual, was at the Earl's Court Boat Show, answering questions, signing autographs and posing for photographs. Late in the afternoon, when the queue had

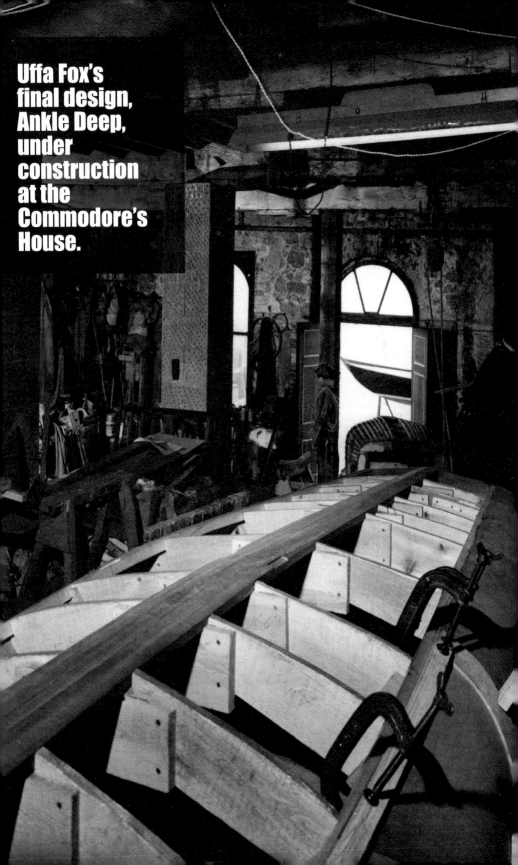

Uffa Fox's final design, Ankle Deep, under construction at the Commodore's House.

subsided, a young man approached and said he wanted to row the Atlantic single-handed. Uffa stared at him for a moment, peering above the gold-rimmed spectacles he wore for reading. He was used to practical jokers and those simply asking daft questions and wasn't sure if this was a serious proposition or not. 'Row the Atlantic single-handed, eh? And what on earth makes you think you can do that, my boy?'

'Mr Fox, I don't need the earth to tell me what I can do, I know.' Uffa paused again; this was the sort of answer he might have given himself, when he was younger. A few questions later he had established that John Fairfax had no money, no backers and no boat. He didn't even know how to row. All the same, there was something about him which suggested he might be serious. Most experts would have sent Fairfax away with a few words of advice, but Uffa had spent his whole life doing things that others said were impossible, and he liked the cut of this young man's jib. The elder statesman of yacht design was nothing if not impulsive, decisive and brave.

'I know exactly what kind of boat you want,' Uffa said, 'and I will design her for you.'

Based on the concept of the Airborne Lifeboat, *Britannia* was twenty-two feet at the waterline with a four-foot-nine-inch beam and a displacement of 1,860 pounds. While she was being constructed, Fairfax practised for several hours per day by rowing across the Serpentine in Hyde Park (hardly a realistic substitute for the Atlantic). *Britannia* was launched from Lallow's boatyard in Cowes on a windy, rainswept day, and Uffa, who was by now in poor health, wrapped himself in oilskins for the event. John Fairfax got in and immediately stowed the oars the wrong way round, then he put them in the gate back to front. When he finally started to row, he struggled with the sliding seat, having never used one before. A journalist commented, 'It's going to need to be a bloody good boat!' That journalist, however, and many other sceptics, were forced to eat their words when Fairfax became the first

John Fairfax, in *Britannia*, became the first solo oarsman
to cross an ocean.

lone oarsman in history to traverse any ocean, successfully
crossing the Atlantic in 180 days. Three years later, Fairfax and
his girlfriend, Sylvia Cook, would become the first persons to
row the Pacific in *Britannia II*, also designed by Uffa.

By 1972, Uffa's health had significantly worsened. During
Cowes Week of that year, he insisted on attending several
events, but often had to rely on a wheelchair. Before the racing
began, he spent a final hour aboard *Coweslip* and took the
helm for the last time. Prince Philip arranged for him to be
winched aboard *Britannia*—he was no longer able to mount
the gangway—and Uffa was moved to tears by the gesture. He
had once said of Philip, 'You could put your heart in his hand
and know it would be cared for.'

Uffa won his last race at the age of seventy, but later that year
suffered a heart attack which robbed him of what little agility he
retained. When he could sail no longer, he designed and built
his final boat, *Ankle Deep*, an outboard-powered launch which
could be raised and lowered from the davits of the Commodore's
House and easily skippered by a man with less and less mobility.
Today, she is preserved at the Classic Boat Museum Boat Shed
in Cowes, along with many of Uffa's other designs.

Uffa with Ankle Deep, the last boat he designed.

When you want to know something
worth knowing, *ask a happy man.*
Here's one. Designs yachts and races them.
Lives, works and welcomes
you in a one-time warehouse,
with a view from the windows like a
sailor's dream of heaven.
Come and meet him . . .

Can we walk in?

ou're in!—so make yourselves comfortable.
ush those photos out of the way. Don't sit
the motor horn. Will you have a Martini?

Thanks!

ait, now . . . Come over here and watch the
ueen Elizabeth go by. I was out there myself
hour ago, in my own Fresh Breeze.
eenty-tonner . . . How do you like it?

Beautiful!

mean the Martini. Maybe that's what you
ean. Straight vermouth, or a little gin?

Straight, please.

raight as a bat! Many's the game of cricket
e played, bang in the middle of the Solent, out
a patch of sand there when the sea's right . . .
raight and dry is my liking. Get the
ste better. And if there's a better taste
an Martini on a fine, bright morning in
wes, my name's not Uffa Fox!

Better drink

ARTINI

weet or Dry

UFFA – Yachting's Eccentric Genius

In the final year of his life, Uffa completed the second volume of his autobiography, *More Joys of Life* (a third book had been planned but was never completed). 'Autobiography' is a loose term; it is really a series of lightly connected essays on events in his life, boats he designed and people he knew. In the final pages, he sums up his highly personal philosophy of life with his own version of the Ten Commandments—which bear almost no resemblance to those he would have learned as a child. They are so idiosyncratic and entertaining—but simultaneously heartfelt—that they are worth reporting in full:

> These ten commandments which I have obeyed will, I believe, enable all to keep healthy and well enough to enjoy everything in life to the full:

> 1. Regular bowel action at least once in every 24 hours is important. Continued cheerfulness is a sign of great wisdom, but dolefulness is a sign of constipation. Just as a coal fire burns brightly if fed with the right amount of fuel, is well poked at regular intervals, and the ashes and clinker are taken away as required, so is a human being all the better for being well fed and cleared out regularly. The great aids to regular clearance are green vegetables, fruit and liquid. Some human beings need, in addition, medicines to keep them going regularly; these should be kind and gentle in their action, as those with a scouring effect are upsetting to the nervous system.

> 2. Always when you can, never when you must. We should always endeavour to keep the bladder empty and comfortable, and remember that we can only drain off three quarters of its contents at a time, so we should make water about a quarter of an hour before bedtime, then again immediately before jumping into bed. Before going on a journey, whether by car, train or horse, we should attend to this matter, as we never know when we will get the next opportunity. Also, if there is an accident, an empty bladder is less likely to burst than a full one.

3. Enjoy sunshine, fresh air, and sensible exercise every day. Fresh air and sensible exercise are the most wonderful things for our health and cost nothing except the effort and the time devoted to them. Different ages must take different degrees of exercise.

A child without strength enough to walk must be taken out in a perambulator to enjoy fresh air and sunshine and the gentle bouncing about of the perambulator frees wind, solids and liquids by keeping them on the move, so without any exertion the baby is exercised and receives fresh air and sunshine.

At the latter end of our life, if we have lived long enough to outgrow our strength in wind and limb, we are then pushed about in a Bath chair with the same effect.

Between these two ages exercise is taken to suit our strength and ability. Swimming, football, cricket, cross-country running, tennis, golf, hunting, shooting, fishing, skiing, sailing—there are a thousand and one sports, pastimes and games ranging from the violent and brutal exercises such as boxing, down through to the gentle, giggly fun of croquet.

4. Eat the minimum of fried foods, have these cooked in a vegetable oil, and never cook in an oven where gas jets are in direct contact with food. Too much frying gums up the system and gives us indigestion, and using animal fats has a harmful effect, so we should fry as little as possible and when we do, use a vegetable oil. We should grill everything possible-— bacon, sausages, kidneys, fish, steaks, chops, and try to fry only the eggs to go with them as these are non-absorbent.

When we cook food in an ordinary oven with a coal range or an Aga cooker, the oven itself is sealed off and entirely separated from the flame and gases; the heat goes round and round without entering it. But all the gas stoves I have seen have the jets and flames in the oven itself and this means that some of the gas can get into the food being cooked therein. We all know that gas is poisonous and, if only one jet is unlit during the cooking, the gas from it could have a harmful effect on the stomach.

5. Never use aluminium cooking utensils unless they are coated inside. Aluminium is a metal that wastes away rapidly in salt water and most foods cooked need salt in the water. This means that by using aluminium saucepans and cooking pans we are continually feeding our insides with aluminium, and once we have overloaded our stomachs with it, it has a harmful effect upon our health and well-being.

Many years ago my inside was rebellious and ill, a state of things brought about by overwork, a great deal of worry, too many late hours, too much drinking and aluminium cooking.

It was decided that I would have an operation and my gall bladder removed; then Arthur Ransome, a great author, sent me a telegram which said,

'Do away with your aluminium cooking things and you won't need this operation.'

I could not believe there was such a simple way out as I had already fixed up the time and place of the operation and that Admiral Wakeley, Head of the Royal College of Surgeons, should perform it. He was such a great surgeon that students watched his operations, so I arranged with him that, if the audience applauded when he was already in my engine room, and he had to do an encore, he could take out my appendix, so all was set.

However, to please my friend I eliminated the aluminium kettle and teapot which we used every afternoon for tea at the office and in their stead used a tinned copper kettle and china teapot.

After three days I stopped feeling sick after tea, as I usually did, and as I was still unable to believe this miracle, I brought the aluminium tea things into use again, and once more felt sick after three days. We repeated this several times, always with the same effect, but, still not believing it, I asked for my tea to be brought in to my own room without being told in what it had been brewed, but that whatever they did they must keep the same kettles and teapots going three days in a row for it to have any effect. The answer was always the same. Therefore I did away with all my aluminium cooking things and my inside improved until after a day with eight hours in the saddle of a horse out hunting, trotting, cantering, galloping and jumping hedges, ditches and fences, I realized I was fit and well again. So I wrote to tell Admiral Wakeley of this day with the Isle of Wight hounds and he agreed that there was no need for him to stick his knife in me. He wrote back, 'I quite agree with you.' So I never had the operation and as I have kept clear of aluminium cooking, I have kept well ever since.

6. Eat and enjoy the right amount of wholesome food at regular intervals every day. When we are young our parents are careful to give us good food at regular intervals, but from twenty to forty, when we have reached our full strength and are in command of our own lives, we constantly abuse our bodies by going without food for too long a period and then eating unsuitable things.

Roast beef or grilled beef steaks are wholesome foods and also nourishing, and I am a believer in eating all the beef possible in the form of roasts, grills, casseroles, stews and so on. Veal is the flesh of a calf that has been hung up and slowly bled white, all its goodness drained out of it, so is, to my mind, a pure waste of time to eat. It is hard to digest and so tasteless that it must always be gingered up with herbs or spices and is without nourishment. It is, in fact, just like kissing your sister.

So we should try to have wholesome, strengthening food at regular hours every day. A breakfast, a midday meal, a refreshing cup of tea about four-thirty, and a good dinner in the cool of the evening, as well balanced and sensible food gives us strength and energy and also keeps our bowel action regular.

Garlic should have a constant place in our diet as it is an

internal disinfectant. 'An apple a day keeps the doctor away, an onion a day keeps the women away' ... and garlic is stronger than either!

There is a little Isle of Wight couplet that runs:

And when to the age of forty we come,
The men go to belly, and the women to bum.

At the age of forty we cease to take the amount of physical exercises we did previously, but continue to eat the same amount of food, and any excess of food over our requirement causes us to spread abroad, then taking less and less exercise while still eating the same quantity, get even thicker aft. Doctor friends of mine who relieved prisoner of war camps in Japan and other places never saw a fat person in any of them, so an easy way to get thin is to ease up on eating and drinking until we become thinner and then continue eating only the right amount.

7. Only take two aperitifs before a meal but drink as much as sensible through and after the meal. As we grow older our education and tastes in foods and wines broadens and we get a great liking for them. As by now we have lost some of our strength in wind and limb we cannot get the wonderful exhilaration and joy we used to get in our younger days from health-giving games and sports such as cricket, football, jumping, so we tend to get our enjoyment from food and drink; I have known some people take such a joy in eating caviar that they become gluttons.

A story I have known since choir boy days was quite new to all the officers, with their Naval Attaché, on a Russian battleship. I told it to them when we were on the sea in a wardroom so large that there were three different tables, so I had to tell it three different times. All of them laughed their heads off.

A man had a friend who loved caviar so much that he

became a glutton for it and, to cure his friend, he invited him to his country house for dinner and the night. In one bowl was the normal amount of caviar for two people which was divided between them, but another and larger bowl was filled with number four shot, cut from a great many 12-bore cartridges and mixed in a black paste of the same taste. The glutton proceeded to devour the whole of this bowl of shot thinking it was caviar.

Dinner went on well and throughout the evening nothing untoward happened, the night too passed peacefully and the next morning the host was amazed to see his friend arrive at the breakfast table looking healthy and well.

He asked, 'Did you have a good night?'

The friend replied, 'Yes, I slept very well indeed and enjoyed my morning bath, but I am sorry to say that on the way downstairs as I bent down to tie up my shoelace, I accidentally shot your dog.'

We must beware of the things we choose in the afternoon of our lives to replace the joy of sport of our younger days. Nothing can ever replace the feeling of exaltation when the cricket ball goes cleanly off your bat, straight out of the field, for a six, so we find fun and consolation after a good meal in a mellow port which gives us a sense of wellbeing that, in a way, replaces the exhilaration and joy we felt when we had excelled in some form of sport in our youth. But we must beware of enjoying the feeling of wellbeing from wines and other luxuries, for having the power to keep on drinking we can overindulge, and overindulgence in anything changes it from a blessing to a curse.

A sensible law for any human is not to have more than two drinks before a meal, then to drink wines throughout the meal and afterwards a liqueur that suits the state of his health, the food, the country he is in and the weather.

What ruins a dinner, a stomach and health, is too many drinks going into an empty stomach before the meal; this also ruins the tummy. It can sometimes delay a meal and as all foods require a certain period of cooking to reach perfection and are spoilt by being over cooked and being kept hot.

When the sun is north of the equator between the Vernal and Autumnal Equinox (from March 21st to September 21st in the northern hemisphere), we can eliminate breakfast, but in winter weather, from dinner in the evening until midday the following day is too long a period between meals.

8. Never mix drinks or drink more than the body enjoys. A mixture of drink is a bad thing as it bewilders and upsets the stomach, so we should therefore stick to one sort of drink. We should keep to drinks made from the grape or from hop or from the different corns and not mix them all up in our inside at the same time.

The right drink at the right moment and the right amount of it is good for us and has been so from the earliest times.

Drink is only harmful when we take it to excess or at wrong times. It is quite sensible to have a couple of sherries before a meal and white and red, still or sparkling, wines through it and port or brandy or liqueurs made from grapes afterwards, as all are produced from the same source; or to drink beer before and through a meal and after it, or perhaps whiskey throughout; but it is bad policy to mix them.

9. Do not drink alcohol within twelve hours of ceasing to drink it the night before. Our insides are so wonderfully made and well balanced that if only we give them a chance they will purify the system of all the poisons poured into them in the way of excess alcohol within twelve hours.

During my lifetime I have seen strong men destroy their health through drink, I have also had friends who drank a great deal and came to no harm. The difference between the two was that the second set of men never drank in the forenoon, and so gave their insides the 12 hours needed to cleanse the system from the impurities left within from the previous night, before starting to drink again, whereas those who destroyed themselves drank morning, noon and night, so their bodies were never free of alcohol.

So, if we stop drinking at two in the morning we should not, in order to have the twelve hours for purification, drink again until after two o'clock the following afternoon, which generally means we shall not be drinking again until six or seven in the evening.

None so pure as the purified.

10. Never stand when you can sit and never sit when you can lie. Hearts pump the blood round our system 24 hours a day, every moment of our lives, day and night, as the moment it stops, time with us is no more.

Because of this we must rest the heart whenever we can by easing up the burden it bears. When a man is standing the heart beats pump a column of blood six feet high, when he sits in a low chair the column is three foot (only half as) high, and when he lays down the blood flows along through level arteries and veins without any pressure through height, which is why sleep is so refreshing. During our eight hours of peaceful sleep every night the heart, although still beating approximately sixty times a minute and pumping blood round the body, is also resting as it now only has to keep the blood in motion along horizontal arteries.'[169]

When the 1972 Cowes Week was over, Uffa's close friends, Norman and Josephine Terry, took him back to their home in Worcestershire where they could nurse him through the final weeks of his life. He managed, with difficulty, to attend the Yachtsman of the Year dinner in London, but it was the last time he would be seen in public. He died on 27 October at the age of seventy-four.

---

169   Recent research has linked sitting for long periods with health problems, including obesity, increased blood pressure, high blood sugar, excess body fat around the waist and unhealthy cholesterol levels. Too much sitting and prolonged periods of sitting also seem to increase the risk of cardiovascular disease and cancer.

(above) Uffa in the mess kit of
the Royal London Yacht Club.

(opposite) One of Uffa's
innovations was the use of a
saddle for the helmsman.

Cowes' Trinity Church was full to capacity for his funeral, and a lesson was read by his close friend, Sir Max Aitken. A London memorial service, held at St Martin-in-the-Fields, saw the church overflowing and among the mourners were Prince Philip, Princess Anne and the Prime Minister, Edward Heath.

He had often said that he did not want to look down from heaven and see an unspent five pounds in his bank account, and his wish was granted; he died as he had lived, with unpaid bills, and—according to Probate Office records—he left no will. During his last years, Norman and Josephine Terry had bought the Commodore's House from him with an agreement that he could live there for the rest of his life, but that money had long gone. Nevertheless, his reputation not only as a designer and builder of exceptional boats, but also as a polymath with a hundred talents, would last long after his debts had been forgotten. His were big shoes to fill and—in the decades that followed—no one really has.

In 2022—the fiftieth anniversary of Uffa's death—the UF50 festival was held in Cowes to commemorate his life. Half a century is long enough for history to form a view, if not—in most instances—to forget an individual altogether. In Uffa's case, his reputation has grown, rather than diminished, in the years since his death. The festival produced an extraordinary response. Dozens of owners of Uffa-designed boats brought them to Cowes to be displayed on The Parade, and many were raced in a regatta organised by the Royal London Yacht Club. A splendidly renovated *Vigilant*, along with examples of Uffa's Firefly, National Twelve, International Fourteen, Redwing, Albacore, National Eighteen, Jolly Boat, Flying Fifteen, Fox Eighteen, Fox Twenty-Four and Atalanta were proudly shown by their owners; many had been restored, many are still raced, but all were wonderful to see. A new generation was spellbound by Uffa's ingenious designs and exquisite workmanship. *Coweslip*, the royal Flying Fifteen, was brought back to her old home—the quay at the Commodore's House—and exhibited to the public. It was a moving tribute, and Uffa would have loved every minute of it.

Weston Martyr made a telling point when he described his old friend as a genius. Uffa Fox was—beyond any reasonable doubt—the best yacht designer of his generation and, arguably, any generation. Genius is not an exaggeration and Martyr was right again when he said we cannot judge such a prodigy by the standards of ordinary mortals. Eccentricity may not be the cause of genius, but it is a common effect, and Uffa's eccentricities were closely linked to his character. He was devoid of the inhibitions and fear of failure which constrain most of us—he always said exactly what he thought and never hesitated to criticise what he knew to be imperfect. He was physically, mentally, and emotionally brave which meant—once he had seen a path to success—he pursued it without any fear of danger or unhappy consequences. His eye for what he called the 'loveliness' of his environment, undoubtedly informed his designs, as did his remarkable head for figures and his photographic memory. His love of nature was more than a sensitivity to beauty; it sprang from a passion that knew no bounds. If ever a man lived life to the full, and knew all of its highs and lows, it was Uffa. The Computer Age—which he so mistrusted—has now been with us for many decades. It has created countless wonders of communication, technology and science, but it has produced few Universal Men and none like Uffa.

Acknowledgements

Nothing is more valuable to a biographer than the personal memories of those who knew the subject. I have been fortunate to speak to many such people. In fact, I was overwhelmed by the response when I first began my research. I am especially grateful to Mike Dixon who—along with his father Tony—is the custodian of a substantial archive of photographs, plans and other documents which belonged to Uffa Fox. Mike not only answered my many questions, but also patiently scanned scores of images and documents for me, many of which are featured in the book.

Several people granted me lengthy interviews including Rodney Barton, Rosemary Joy, Andy Cassell, Cindy Betley and, once again, Mike Dixon. I am also grateful to Mark McNeill, Diana McNeill, Graham Caulfield, Claire Gregory, Wendy Owens, The East Cowes Heritage Centre, the Classic Boat Museum, Cowes Corinthian Yacht Club and Cowes Library. I hope I have done Uffa justice, I certainly couldn't have without your help.

Bibliography

Boothroyd, Basil. *Prince Philip: An Informal Biography.* McCall. 1971.

Dixon, June. *UFFA FOX: A Personal Biography.* Angus & Robertson. 1978.

Fox, Uffa. *According to Uffa.* Newnes. 1960.

Fox, Uffa. *Joys of Life.* Newnes 1966.

Fox, Uffa. *More Joys of Living.* Nautical Publishing Company. 1972.

Fox, Uffa, *Sailing, Seamanship and Yacht Construction,* Peter Davies, 1934.

Fox, Uffa. *Sailing Boats.* Newnes. 1959.

Lloyd, Ian. *The Duke.* The History Press. 2021.

Mills, A D. *The Place-Names of the Isle of Wight.* Paul Watkins Publishing. 1966.

Nutting, William Washburn. *The Track of the Typhoon.* Motor Boat Publishing. New York. 1922.

Parker, Eileen. *Step Aside for Royalty.* Chris Moore. 1982.

Scott, Peter. *The Eye of the Wind.* Hodder & Stoughton. 1967.

Taylor, J W R. *A Short History of Saunders-Roe.* 1960.

Thompson, Paul. *Sea-Change—Wivenhoe Remembered.* The History Press. 2006.

Index

Adriana (schooner) 58
Airborne Lifeboat, 144–153, 155, 160, 162–187
Aitken, Max, 31, 127, 214, 244
Aitken, Violet, 215
Albacore (dinghy), 224
Albert, Prince, 16, 22, 203
Ankle Deep, 231
Anne, Princess, 217, 244
Ariel (dinghy), 65, 68
Atalanta (yacht), 210, 245
Atkey, Bruce, 70
Atkey, Cecil, 70
Avenger (dinghy), 9, 76–87
Avro Lancaster, 162

Baden-Powell, Robert, 32
Baden-Powell, Warrington, 32
Bader, Douglas, 220–222
Baltimore Sun, 204
Barrie, J M, 103–104
Barton George, 128, 223
Barton, Rodney, 130, 223–224

Beaton, Cecil, 106-107
Beatrice, Princess 22
Beaverbrook, Lord, 128, 146, 214
Bee, The (ship), 24
Beken of Cowes, 108–109
Bell, Isaac (Ikey), 113–114
Bembridge Redwing (dinghy), 145
Bembridge Sailing Club, 63
Bermuda Cup, 58
Betley, Cindy, 217
Black Rose (schooner), 10, 89–90
Blackwood's Magazine, 164
Blint, Billie, 38
Bloodhound (yacht), 113
Bluebottle (yacht), 7
Boat Racing Association (BRA), 63
Brabazon, John Moore, 145–146
Brading, Arthur, 38, 112
Britannia (rowing boat), 230–231

Index

Britannia II (rowing boat), 231
British India Steam Navigation Company, 41

Camper & Nicholsons, 64, 113
Cassell, Andy, 224
Caulfield, Graham, 218
Chandler, Bill, 198
Charles III, King, 122, 220
Churchill, Winston, 128, 145, 163
Classic Boat Museum, 231
Colman, Alan, 111–112, 115
Columbine (boat), 36
Commodore's House, 127, 204, 207, 213–214, 219, 222, 244
Cook, Sylvia, 231
Cooke Alastair, 204
Cooke, R T, 92
Corry, Brian, 163
Cowes Blitz, 142
Cowes Corinthian Yacht Club, 224
Cowes Torquay Offshore Powerboat Race, 214
Coweslip (yacht), 7, 194, 207–208, 231, 245
Crews, Stanley (Spike), 54, 57, 80, 224
Cunliffe Owens, 148

Dad's Army, 140
Daily Express, 215
Dainty Duck (*see* Flying Fifteen)
Damant, James (Jimmy), 7, 202
Daring, Dinghy, 87
Davies, Peter Lewellyn, 105–108, 113, 133
de Quincy, Roger, 103
Diablesse (yacht), 58–60
Dickerson, Bob, 57, 80, 92, 147
Dimbleby, Richard, 220
Dixon, June, 136–137, 140, 187
Dixon, Peter, 134
Dixon, Tony, 7, 16, 41
Dollery, Clive, 210
Dorade (yacht), 99
Dorset, Jim, 44, 46
du Maurier, Daphne, 105

East Cowes Sailing Club, 130
Edinburgh, Duke of, 7–9, 28, 122, 203–205, 207–209, 212, 217, 225, 231, 244
Edward VII, King, 18
Edward VIII, King, 205
Elizabeth II, Queen, 7, 8, 203
Esmeralda (ship), 14

Fairey Aviation Group, 187, 210
Fairey Marine (*see* Fairey
    Aviation Group)
Fairfax, John 230
Fleet Air Arm 146
Floating Bridge, 72–76, 82,
    88, 117
Flying Fifteen 7, 10, 191–
    196, 202, 224
Flying Twenty-Five, 189
Folly Regatta, 128–130
Forsham, John, 220
Fox, Alma (née Phillips),
    68–69, 74–75, 86, 100,
    108, 133–134
Fox, Arthur, 13, 16, 19,
    25–26, 38, 41, 44, 56–57,
    69, 73, 134, 136, 154,
    157–158
Fox, Cherry (see Laura Fox)
Fox, Dorothea, 12
Fox, Elfrida 12, 134, 136, 157
Fox, Eliza (née Cobbold),
    15–16, 18, 23, 154
Fox, Elizabeth (née
    Roberton), 14
Fox, Herbert, 12
Fox, John, 14
Fox, Laura Louisa (née
    Enoch), 133–134, 136,
    155, 186, 188–189

Fox, Lucy (*see* Eliza Fox)
Fox, Mahala, 12, 14
Fox, Mary Jane, 14
Fox, Yvonne, 210–213, 217,
    224
Francki, Wojciech, 142–143
Frantic (horse) 158–160
Freemasons, 154

General Municipal and
    Boilermakers Society
    (GMB), 67
George Marvin & Son, 32,
    34, 55
George VI, King, 9, 12,
    200–201, 203
Goatley, Fred 38
Goldfish Club, 163
Goodwin, Ron, 127
Gregory, Claire, 217, 219
Groves and Gutteridge, 147
Guillem Sorolla (ship), 47

Hammond, Paul, 97, 99
Handley Page Halifax, 162
Harmsworth Cup, 36
Hawker Typhoon, 160
Heath, Edward, 208, 217,
    244

Index

Hillyer, William, 17
HMS *Avenger*, 14
HMS *Wessex*, 204
HMY *Alberta*, 18
HMY *Britannia*, 24–25, 75, 202, 204–205, 207–208, 213, 217
Home Guard, 139–140
Hookey, Charley, 42, 48
Hore-Ruthven, Alison, 106–107
Hore-Ruthven, Margaret, 106-107
Humbert, A J, 22

Illustrated London News, 14
Island Sailing Club (ISC), 63–64

Jackman, Ronald, 30
Jolly Boat, 210, 244
Joy, Rosemary, 219–220
Justice, James Robertson, 205

Keeping, Arthur (Buster), 85–86
Kelley, Ann, 59
Kelley, John B, 58

Lallow, Clare, 83
Lamport and Holt Line, 49
Landfall (yacht), 97–99
Leif Eriksson (yacht), 48
Lidstone, Harry, 32
Local Defence Volunteers (*see* Home Guard)
Lockheed Hudson, 144, 146–150, 162
London Boat Show, 215, 227
Looe Redwing (dinghy) 111
Looe Sailing Club, 111
Lowe, Dave, 210
Luftwaffe, 142–143
Lumberjack (schooner), 127

Macmillan, Harold, 207
Maple Leaf IV (boat), 36, 66–67
Martin, George, 127
Martyr, Weston, 120, 163, 245
Marvin, Eric, 156
McGregor, John, 102
McQueen Mason, John 130
Medina House, 131, 136, 138–139, 144, 155
Medina Yard, 131, 138, 140–141
Mew, Lenny, 124, 128

Mike Sammes Singers, 128
Miller, Joe, 14
Morgan-Giles, Frank, 63–66, 68, 70, 108
Morning Cloud (yacht), 208
Mountbatten, Louis, 205
Mountbatten, Philip, (*see* Duke of Edinburgh)
My Dainty Duck (yacht), 7

Nahum, Baron, 205
New York Canoe Club, 103
New York Tribune, 42
Nicholson, Charles, 63
Nutting, William Washburn (Bill), 42–44, 47, 61, 99

Olaf, Prince, 93
ORP *Błyskawica*, 142–144
Owers Lightvessel, 84

Parker, Eileen, 204, 207
Parker, Michael, 197, 204, 207, 220, 222, 225
Parkhust Prison, 127
Pensive Temptress (yacht) 189–190

Peter Pan, 103–104
Philip, Prince, (*see* Duke of Edinburgh)
Pollock, Brian, 127
Porter, S E (Joe), 38
Prince of Wales Cup, 9, 70, 80, 87, 90–91, 102
Puckaster, 155–161, 186, 197, 199–201

Radiant (dinghy), 70
Ramsay, Eileen, 214
Ratsey & Lapthorn, 61, 201
Ratsey, Chris, 61, 64
RMS *Celtic*, 48
RMS *Empress of Britain*, 103
Rogerson, J W, 23, 28
Royal Air Force (RAF), 40, 138, 148, 214
Royal Corinthian Yacht Club, 212
Royal London Yacht Club (RLYC), 31, 244
Royal Naval Air Service (RNAS), 36, 39–40
Royal Society for the Prevention of Cruelty to Animals (RSPCA), 67
Royal Society of Arts, 225

Index

Royal Thames Yacht Club (RTYC), 197–198
Royal Yacht Squadron (RYS), 203
Royal Yachting Association (RYA), 63
Royce, Charles, 145
Ruthven, Lord, 106–107, 133
RYA Firefly (dinghy), 188, 196, 244

Sach, Bobbie, 136, 138–139, 186
Saunders, S E (Sam), 35–37, 39, 41, 66, 102, 117–118
Savage, Bob, 27, 128, 130
Scott, Peter, 39, 63, 66, 134, 224
Shakespeare, Willam, 21
Shipconstructors' and Shipwrights' Association (SSA), 67
Short Stirling, 162
Slessor, John, 222
Smith, Spot, 35, 54
Smythe, Pat, 218
Société des Regattes du Havre, 82
Somerset, Bobby, 58–59

Sopwith, Thomas (Tommy), 36
SS *Roman Prince*, 48
SS Swallow, 54
SS *Vauban*, 49
St Martin-in-the-Fields, 244
Stephens, Olin, 99
Sweisguth, Francis, 189

Terry, Josephine, 225, 241, 244
Terry, Norman, 241, 244
Thames Ironworks, 41
The Wind in the Willows, 121
This Is Your Life, 58, 224
Thomas, Bill, 160
Thornycroft, Tom 84, 190
Thursday Club, 205
Toad of Toad Hall, 121
Tom and Jerry, 217
Trinity Church, Cowes, 244
Twenty Acres, 120–122, 133–134, 155, 157
Typhoon (yacht) 42–47, 49, 58

Uffa Sings Sea Shanties, 128

Valhalla (ship), 27, 34
Vamarie (yacht), 112
Vaughan, Tom, 79
Vickers Warwick, 162–163, 179
Victoria, Queen, 14, 16, 73, 208
Vigilant (yacht), 92–97, 244
Vince, Ernie, 115

Waight, Bill, 39, 50, 57–60, 111, 139, 192, 224
Ward, Stephen, 207
Warren, Archie, 158
Westbourne House, 131, 144

White, Eric, 32
White, Harry, 32
White, J S (shipyard), 14, 58, 85, 142, 224
Willis, Charles, 112
Willoughby, Vera 103–104
Wingham, Harry, 8, 140
Wishbone (yacht), 112–116

Yacht Racing Association (YRA), 63
Yachting Monthly, 64
Yachts and Yachting, 97
Yates, Charlie, 226

SunRise

Star Turns

ger Moore Susannah York Claire Bloom Quenti
lly Goodwin Peter Bowles Sean Connery David
ah Miles Ronnie Corbett Peter Ustinov Glenda
ewart Granger Earl... José Ferrer Maggie
a Rigg Gwen Ffrangcon-Davies Julio Iglesias Jo
d Sinden Geraldine James een Atkins Barbar
ie Corbett Charlton Heston Lauren Bacall Sta
Richard Chamberlain Antony Sher Tom
s Schlesinger Tom Wilkinson Ken Dodd ...via A
teiger Malcolm Muggeridge Patrick Stewart Ro
ony Quayle Ronald Harwood Patrick Kielty Ian
Marceau Bernard Dellont Rupert Everett John
... Christopher Lee ... Harbor Anto
n Atkinson Stephen Fry Michael Winner Steph
...wright Frances Barber Quentin Crisp Angela
ff Richard ... Robert Hardy Peter V
rry Andrews Fay Wray Claudia ...by Toby S
chael Horden Vera Lynn Dora Bryan Ian McDi

Tim Walker

'Tim Walker writes such a good, readable book.'
Fay Weldon, Mail on Sunday

Ari, Jackie & Maria
The Pirate, The Princess & The Diva

Onassis, Kennedy, Callas
The Love Triangle of
the 20th Century

Malcolm Turner

Deny & Disavow

The British Empire
in the Culture War

'Incredibly accessible, totally authoritative, and intensely readable.'
Sathnam Sanghera

Alan Lester

AMERICAN OBSESSION

Howard Hughes &
Juan Trippe:
Rivals in the Sky

Peter Pigott

www.sunpub.info